Harvard
Business
Review
ON
BREAKTHROUGH
LEADERSHIP

THE HARVARD BUSINESS REVIEW PAPERBACK SERIES

The series is designed to bring today's managers and professionals the fundamental information they need to stay competitive in a fast-moving world. From the preeminent thinkers whose work has defined an entire field to the rising stars who will redefine the way we think about business, here are the leading minds and landmark ideas that have established the *Harvard Business Review* as required reading for ambitious businesspeople in organizations around the globe.

Other books in the series:

Harvard Business Review

ON

BREAKTHROUGH

LEADERSHIP

A HARVARD BUSINESS REVIEW PAPERBACK

The *Harvard Business Review* articles in this collection are available as individual reprints. Discounts apply to quantity purchases. For information and ordering, please contact Customer Service, Harvard Business School Publishing, Boston, MA 02163. Telephone: (617) 783-7500 or (800) 988-0886, 8 A.M. to 6 P.M. Eastern Time, Monday through Friday. Fax: (617) 783-7555, 24 hours a day. E-mail: custserv@hbsp.harvard.edu

Library of Congress Control Number: 2002100253

The paper used in this publication meets the requirements of the American National Standard for Permanence of Paper for Publications and Documents in Libraries and Archives Z39.48-1992.

Contents

Harvard Business Review

ON

BREAKTHROUGH

LEADERSHIP

Personal Histories

Leaders Remember the Moments and People That Shaped Them

HARRIS COLLINGWOOD

Executive Summary

IF LEADERSHIP IS PERSONAL, then personal experience must hold some of the most valuable lessons in leadership. With that in mind, HBR's editors canvassed leaders in business, academia, and the arts, asking them to tell us about the experiences that taught them the most about leadership at its best—and worst.

Each of the 17 responses was unique, of course, but some common threads emerged. Many of those we asked credited one or both parents with teaching them principles of good leadership. Several cited their own lapses as examples of bad leadership. Some leaders were transformed by experiences in the military or on the playing fields of school. Others found defining moments in the social movements of the 1960s.

Disney CEO Michael Eisner credits his high school headmaster—a man he didn't even like—with teaching him the importance of striving for excellence and the dangers of insisting on perfection. From his experiences as a young officer aboard a World War II destroyer, former Washington Post editor Ben Bradlee learned the value of hiring people smarter than he is. Both Xerox CEO Anne Mulcahy and Francis Collins, the director of the NIH's National Human Genome Research Institute, credit their parents with teaching them the importance of building consensus. But Semco owner Ricardo Semler says consensus is just a beginning: He draws on Lewis Carroll to suggest that sustained value is created only when managers give up control altogether and let their employees take the lead.

Ultimately, what all these stories demonstrate is that the act of leadership is just that—action. It's about showing, not telling, and setting the right example.

LEADERSHIP, WE'RE OFTEN TOLD, is a matter of setting the right example. It seems logical, then, to ask today's leaders for their defining examples of good and bad leadership. HBR canvassed leaders in business, education, and the arts, posing to each of them two questions: What person, experience, or work of literature taught you the most about effective leadership? What person or experience taught you the meaning of bad leadership?

No two answers were the same, of course, but some intriguing similarities did emerge. Perhaps most notably, leadership began at home for several respondents. They credited one or both parents with teaching them the principles of good leadership. Interestingly, several of those respondents went on to single out lapses of their own as examples of bad leadership. Several other leaders were transformed by their experiences in the military. Still others found their defining moments in the social movements of the 1960s.

Inevitably, the stories gathered here make mention of various leadership principles and philosophies. But they find their expression in deeds, not words. And that may be the most important lesson of all: Ultimately, the act of leadership is just that—action. It's about showing, not telling. It's about setting the right example, after all.

MICHAEL EISNER *is the chairman and CEO of Disney in Burbank, California.*

I was a typical testing-type teenager; challenging authority seemed to be my goal. So, of course, my most valuable lesson in leadership came from my greatest, and at the time most-resisted, authority figure—Bruce McClellan, the head of my high school. Interspersed among his consistent reminders that he had authority and I didn't was the constant admonition that whatever you do, do it with excellence. This sounded like a cliché then, and it sounds like one now. But sometimes clichés are worth listening to. Mr. McClellan trumpeted his search-for-excellence motto thousands of times during my three years in his vocal presence. I was too proud and too rebellious to admit I was listening. Sports and getting through school were my main goals. But, always, there was the undercurrent of his credo of excellence. If you were playing intramural soccer, or if you were making a cheeseburger, or if you were cutting the grass, his theory was: Don't screw around; do it with excellence.

I heard this line at school so many times I mocked it. If I fouled out in a basketball game, I blocked it from my thoughts. If I didn't study and got an average grade, I ignored it. If I forgot my sister's birthday and quickly bought a thoughtless gift, I misunderstood it. But deep down, his words, his repetition of that quest for excellence, his passion for doing it better, stuck with me. And as I became less of an adolescent, those words from Bruce McClellan started to make sense, the way calculus or organic chemistry or Shakespeare finally make sense.

Here's the best part: If you strive for excellence, you may not always succeed at leading, but you will certainly succeed at living.

They made sense because excellence was the only way to avoid the harsh abyss of mediocrity. Of course I didn't realize that until sometime later, maybe after my first failure as an executive at ABC.

Imperceptibly, Mr. McClellan's advice went from annoying to inspirational, the foundation for just about all I've accomplished. And, at some point, I learned not to confuse "excellence" with "perfection." Perfection is unattainable. But excellence is achievable with enough concerted effort. You just can't ever let up.

And here's the best part of Mr. McClellan's directive. If you strive for excellence, you may not always succeed at leading, but you will certainly succeed at living. If you keep your eye on the ball of excellence, you will find fulfillment, whether you have an army of followers in your wake or you are alone, confidently striding down a solitary path.

PERCY BARNEVIK *is the chairman and former CEO of ABB in Zurich, Switzerland.*

The person who taught me the most about leadership was Hans Werthén. He ran Electrolux from 1967 to 1991, acquiring some 100 companies and making the Swedish corporation into the world's biggest producer of household appliances. I didn't work for him, but he was kind of a mentor for me. He was extremely determined and forceful, and he drove his people hard to accomplish what he wanted to get done. But they were very loyal to him because he somehow was able to combine an iron-fist style with a positive and enjoyable atmosphere. He was just plain fun to work with—very down to earth, ironic about himself, always ready to dissolve tensions with a joke. Contrast him with those macho managers who show up on those "toughest managers in the U.S." lists. In my view, their approach is wrong. The tougher the work you have to do, the more compassionate you have to be.

DANIEL GOLDIN *is the administrator of NASA in Washington, DC.*

My father marched to the beat of a different drummer. We never had much money, so he built the family car out of parts we scavenged from the junkyard. At the time, cars were sedate dark colors. He painted our car sky blue. We called it Lou's Blue Streak. I was embarrassed, but he didn't worry about what anyone thought.

My father encouraged me to read widely and deeply, and he also insisted that I appreciate music. On Saturdays, when my friends were playing ball or were at the movies, I listened to Milton Cross and the Metropolitan Opera, whether or not I wanted to. I complained at the time, but now I see that my father was teaching me to handle a multiplicity of information. When you're running a large, complex organization, there's a temptation to seek order and calm and peace. But creativity doesn't come from seeking stability; it comes from sorting through large, complex inputs and prioritizing them. My father taught me not to allow the chaos and complexity of things to be an excuse for failure.

I will use myself as an example of bad leadership. When my daughter Laura was two or three, we lived in a garden apartment in Los Angeles on a very busy street. We had a strict rule that the front gate was to be closed at all times and that Laura couldn't go into the front yard without a grown-up. Laura never cared much for rules. She would open the gate and play with her friends on the front lawn. I warned her once. I warned her twice. The third time, I grabbed her up with a great deal of anger and spanked her. After that, she would tell her friends, "You'd better not go outside the gate; you'll get a licking."

I realized then that I had broken Laura's spirit, at least a bit. It was a clear example of overreaction. Leaders need to be conscious of the power they wield. I am a very forceful personality and I'm passionate, and sometimes I kind of bowl people over without meaning to. Whenever I catch myself doing it, I apologize.

CHRIS ARGYRIS *is the James Bryant Conant Professor Emeritus of Education and Organizational Behavior at Harvard Business School in Boston. He is also a director of the Monitor Group in Cambridge, Massachusetts.*

One of the most important lessons I learned was from an infantry lieutenant from New York. Most of us who were in the army will remember griping about how hard our assignments were. My lieutenant was quite matter-of-fact about our complaints. "Yes, this is tough," he would reply, "but it's nowhere near what you're going to experience when you go into combat. I'd rather get you prepared than cave in to your complaints." I suppose his kind of uncompromising commitment would be called tough love today. To me it's a powerful reminder that leadership is about maximizing your followers' well-being, not their comfort.

The person who taught me the most about ineffective leadership was myself. Near the end of World War II, I was a Signal Corps officer in charge of a depot. When my tour was nearly over, a woman named Sheila called me out of my office, where about 300 employees had gathered. "Lieutenant," she said, "we just want to tell you what a wonderful boss you have been." Then she hugged and kissed me and gave me a savings bond in an envelope and a beautiful leather bag. I thought I must be a pretty fine leader.

A short while later, I went back to the depot to say hello. The war was over, and the man who was my assistant was now running the place. I said, "Bill, tell me, what did you really think of me as a leader?" And he began to tell me negative things I had never heard before—that I was too competitive, that I didn't give a darn who I rolled over as long as we met the promised goals. I was stunned. Suddenly Sheila came our way. "Sheila," I called out to her, "What Bill is saying about my leadership—is it true?" She looked me straight in the face. "Uh-huh, lieutenant, it sure is," she said. "And one more thing—all of us here are glad that the war finally ended because we were fed up with the act we had to put on for all you officers."

My immediate reaction was, "Oh, my God, this is so unfair." But gradually I realized that whether the feedback was right or wrong was irrelevant—what was relevant was how unaware I had been. That's what got me started on learning about myself and my own blind spots. Eventually, I moved on to the problems of organizations and leadership.

BEN BRADLEE *is the former executive editor of the* Washington Post.

My first experience in leadership came aboard the destroyer USS *Philip* during World War II when I was 21 years old. I became officer of the deck, which meant that on your watch, unless you were in actual battle, you essentially ran the ship. I learned two things that I carried with me, ultimately, into the newsroom of the *Washington Post.*

One is the need to make quick decisions. On a destroyer in wartime, you never know what's going to happen when you wake up in the morning. The same is true in a newsroom. You're putting out five editions a day, and there's virtually an infinite number of ways to fill every column. You have to decide which stories to cover, who's going to write them, how much to mess with what those people have written, where the stories are going to go in the paper. And these decisions cascade down over you by the end of the day as deadlines approach. Major decisions that affect the reputation of the paper have to be made in minutes. It makes Internet time look slow.

The other thing I learned is that you can't make these decisions without good people around you. It was true when I was running a destroyer, and it's just as true in the newspaper business. If you're smart, you'll hire and inspire people who are smarter than you—or at least know more than you do about a lot of things. That makes those difficult decisions you have to make a little easier.

Given the *Post's* history of tough and skeptical journalism, you might expect me to cite numerous examples of bad leadership by presidents over the past half-century. But increasingly I have sympathy for these guys—they really have an impossible job. As I grow older, even Reagan's leadership seems exemplary. He may not have been a rocket scientist, but he was a great leader in bringing this country together.

VICTOR J. MENEZES *is the chairman and CEO of Citibank and a member of the management committee of Citigroup in New York.*

Leadership comes through most in a crisis, and that's what Citibank faced in 1990 and 1991. Our stock price was down to $6, and it wasn't clear whether the bank could survive. That's when John Reed, then the bank's chairman, displayed unusual and outstanding qualities of leadership.

Basically, John focused the bank on a few things and communicated a simple plan to the board, the regulators, and the Street. That struck me as a great example of effective leadership because it galvanized the organization into pulling through. John simplified the extremely complex Citibank organization, made cost cutting a priority, and tied every one of the bank's activities to a set of deliverables. Then, every month, he got the top 15 people together and reviewed how we were doing against the plan.

The interesting thing is, throughout that period we never ever jettisoned a franchise. If you look at the other U.S. banks, most of them got out of their international businesses at that time. Not only did we maintain our international franchise, we grew it. That was one of the simple rules that John formulated and communicated throughout the organization: Shareholders and employees could get hurt, but the customer would not.

ANNE M. MULCAHY *is the president and CEO of Xerox in Stamford, Connecticut.*

I learned some of my most valuable lessons in leadership at the family dinner table, where my father presided over nightly debates with me, my mother, and four brothers. My father, a teacher and writer, knew exactly how to extract independent thinking and creative ideas from all of us. The topics would vary—politics, business, literature, current events, civic issues—but everyone was expected to articulate a position and defend it. If you didn't contribute, you didn't eat, or at least that was the joke. And we didn't just debate; my father encouraged us to turn our words in action.

Bad leadership can happen when you move too fast—or not fast enough—and when you don't bring people into the process of change. Xerox struggled with those issues over the past two years and, frankly, we paid the price. But we have emerged with a greater understanding of what it takes not only to turn the company around but to position it for future growth. When you're in a leadership position, there's nothing like a crisis to help you focus. In many ways, it actually helps you lead and inspires others to rise to the challenge.

JAMES CONLON *is the principal conductor of the Paris Opera and the general music director of the city of Cologne, Germany.*

When I was 12 years old, my father took me to hear Dr. Martin Luther King, Jr., speak at a luncheon in New

York City, and I got to meet him briefly and shake his hand. His dedication, bravery, and altruism were a tremendous inspiration, but it was his death that had the most profound effect on me. I learned the hard lesson that a leader's time is finite and should not be squandered.

King's philosophy was an important antidote for me in two respects. First, it constantly prodded me to go beyond the inborn self-centeredness of the artistic soul. Second, it showed me the power of committing one's life passionately and compassionately to helping others. His vision created spiritual, intellectual, and physical energy that eclipsed the self-defeating negativity that had often accompanied my musical education. Many of my early teachers focused on my imperfections, provoking feelings of inadequacy in me. When I began conducting, I employed some of those negative methods without realizing it, but over several decades I worked hard to shed them. King's inspiration and clear moral vision have helped me throughout my entire professional life to differentiate between depth and superficiality, between the important and the trivial.

ELEANOR M. JOSAITIS *is a cofounder and the executive director of Focus:Hope, a Detroit-based civil and human rights organization.*

I remember, to the exact moment, when my life changed. The year was 1962. I was a 30-year-old housewife, raising five children, living a comfortable life in the suburbs of Detroit. One evening, I was alone at home, watching the Nuremberg trials on television. Suddenly, the program was interrupted by news of the march in Selma, Alabama. I watched as policemen rode through the demonstrators, shocking them with cattle prods, letting dogs loose on them, turning fire hoses on them.

I sat there and cried my eyes out for hours. I kept asking myself: "What would I have done if I had lived in Germany during that prewar time? Would I have pretended that I saw nothing? Would I have become involved?" I also wondered: "What am I doing about what's going on in my own country?" I immediately became a strong supporter of Martin Luther King. Father William Cunningham, an English professor at Sacred Heart Seminary, who was a good friend of mine, was also a strong supporter of Dr. King. When the riots hit Detroit in 1967, Father Cunningham and I came together and said we've got to do something immediately.

If you believe in something and have a passion for it, you have to stand up for it. And you have to be persistent, no matter how long it takes.

My husband, Donald, and I sold our home in the suburbs and moved into an integrated neighborhood in the heart of the city because I was not going to ask anybody to do anything I wasn't going to do myself. I'm still in the same house. My husband was very supportive, but it was not easy. My mother hired an attorney to take my five children away from me. My father-in-law disowned us. My brother-in-law asked me to use my maiden name so I wouldn't embarrass the family. There were difficult times; friendships were broken. At one party, the hostess said, "Hurry up and eat, everybody, because so-and-so has to go to work. He's a police officer, and he has to go and kill the niggers." I just looked at my husband, and we got up and walked out.

I discovered that three things are important to me: passion, persistence, and partnerships. I had a passion for civil rights, but I had to learn the art of persistence. If you believe in something and have a passion for it, you have to stand up for it. And you have to be persistent, no matter how long it takes. I also learned early on that you had better have partners. For the past 33 years, I have surrounded myself with people who share the mission we wrote back on March 8, 1968: intelligent and practical action to overcome racism, poverty, and injustice.

FRANCIS S. COLLINS, MD, *is the director of the National Human Genome Research Institute at the National Institutes of Health in Bethesda, Maryland.*

Whatever leadership skills I have were probably nurtured very early by my parents. Still active in their 90s, my parents founded and developed several groups devoted to theater and the arts in their small town in Virginia. Growing up in the midst of all that creative energy, I had ample opportunity to watch them work their magic: recruiting busy people, drawing them into a shared vision of excellence, and then giving them the responsibility and the freedom to pursue that dream—even reformulate it.

Even when you're sure that you are right, you still shouldn't bypass the step of consensus building.

In the early 1950s, my parents decided to start a summer theater in the grove of oak trees on our farm. Because there was no budget to support this project, my father recruited a small group of men from the neighboring town—lawyers, businessmen, and engineers—all with day jobs. They spent many weekends doing back-breaking work, hauling rocks from the property to build the stage. Every Saturday evening, my parents would have wonderful parties filled with music to celebrate the progress they had made, and that small group of men turned into actors, directors, and producers of everything from Shakespeare to Sondheim. Today, the theater is in its 48th consecutive season and is sold out, as usual.

As for leadership gone awry, I suppose that criticism should begin with oneself. When I first came to the NIH, researchers had made a new but rather tentative discovery about colon cancer. Concerned that the information might be used prematurely, I drafted a statement of caution that my advisory council quickly endorsed. But I had not worked hard enough to build bridges with the medical professional societies that also had a major interest in the issue. Although those societies generally agreed with my statement, their leaders were incensed that the recommendations were coming from the NIH and not from them. It took me several years to repair the damage, and I learned an invaluable lesson: Even when you are sure that you are right and that other knowledgeable experts will probably agree with you, you still shouldn't bypass the step of consensus building. It may be time consuming, but it's vitally important.

JACK WELCH *was the chairman and CEO of General Electric for 20 years. He retired in September.*

Like I've said many times, my mother was the greatest leadership teacher I ever had, even though she was never in a formal leadership position herself. (The truth was, she did "run" the neighborhood.) My mother taught me about unconditional love and, at the same time, set very tough standards for achievement. That combination of "hugs and kicks" brought out the best in me, and I used it myself to bring out the best in others.

After my mother, I think the greatest break in my life was growing up in an atmosphere in which there was a lot of team sports. They taught me that winning is about having the very best people. It doesn't help you if you're surrounded by people who are less talented than you are. You're lucky if your teammates are better and faster than you are, even if you are pretty good. And that's true in business, too. You can't win alone. You just can't.

I was lucky to start a new GE plastics business. I was the first employee; then I hired my first, and a second, and a third. Soon after, we had to ask one of them to leave, which was too bad because we liked him. But we were building the team, and he wasn't good enough. Sports teams do that every day. Why shouldn't business?

When I was a kid, I often wasn't the best player on the team. And when I got to GE, I wasn't always the smartest guy in the room. But I always looked to find the best— people smarter than me. Once I did that, they would take care of the rest. Building their own teams with the best. Every day, I fought to field the very best team. I always believed that was the way to win.

LAURA D'ANDREA TYSON *is the dean of the Haas School of Business at the University of California, Berkeley. In January, she will become the dean of the London Business School.*

I learned most of my leadership skills during my four years of service for President Clinton. The first thing I learned about leadership is the need to be clear about your mission. In my first job, as chair of the Council of Economic Advisers, I was responsible for developing a team of economic experts to advise the president on

economic trends, formulate sound policies, and explain
the administration's strategies to the Congress and to
the citizenry. This job relied on my expertise in eco-
nomics and my communication skills. Then, as NEC
chair, I was charged with organizing a multiagency process to develop economic policy. This job drew heavily
on my skills as a consensus builder and honest broker
as well as on my ability to simplify complicated economic issues.

I learned a lot about effective leadership from Robert
Rubin, who preceded me as NEC chair. He taught me
about the importance of recognizing one's own strengths
and weaknesses. He taught me that a leader earns
respect through humility, not arrogance, and that the
keys to a leader's success are the talent, intelligence, and
loyalty of her team. I have put these lessons to work at
the Haas School, where I have fostered a leadership culture that values expertise and intelligence above rank
and title.

The most dramatic example of bad leadership I can
recall was the politically motivated 1996 decision by the
California Board of Regents to remove considerations of
affirmative action from admissions policies at the University of California. None of the stakeholders of the university—faculty, students, administrators, alumni—
favored this move. Nor was it consistent with the
university's mission to provide access to a diverse group
of qualified students. This year, the regents reversed this
decision in response to sharp declines in applications by
and admissions of qualified minority students. There are
two lessons from this example: Don't let short-term
political concerns shape policy, and don't impose
changes that are not supported by an organization's
stakeholders and are inconsistent with its mission.

RICARDO SEMLER *is the majority owner of Semco in Sao Paulo, Brazil.*

The person who taught me most about leadership was Lewis Carroll. He wrote, "If you don't know where you're going, any road will take you there." This phrase is usually interpreted as a mockery of people who are confused or lack a sense of direction, but I always saw it as positive and illuminating—an assertion of a feminine, intuitive intelligence. Managers overrate knowing where they are going, understanding what business they are in, defining their mission. It is a macho, militaristic, and self-misleading posture. Giving up control in exchange for freedom, creativity, and inspired adaptation is my preference, and Carroll made this apparent to me.

Bad leadership is personified to me by the Pope, Fidel Castro, Bill Gates, and Lee Iacocca, all wonderful figures, brilliant strategists, and historic giants. They created enormous value and transformed the entities they led into some of the most important symbols of our age. But because they couldn't rise above their egos, they failed to create organizations that could flourish in spite of them, not because of them. Because they all overstayed their welcome, they have presided over declining creativity, freedom, innovation, and success. If the organizations they lead are to survive, someone else will have to invent ways to do away with their inheritance. It will be a heavy task.

You have a right only to work, never to the results of that work.

RAJAT GUPTA *is the worldwide managing director of McKinsey & Company in Boston.*

As a philosophy of leadership, Hinduism's Karma Yoga has had the most profound impact on me. In the *Bhagavad Gita,* which is a way of thinking about life, there is a Sanskrit verse that constantly reminds me about the framework of leadership. Translated, it runs, "You have a right only to work, never to the results of that work." To me that means that not only must you do the right thing, but you must do it with the right motives. And you must always do your very best. It was my father who first taught me this idea. He never worried about what the results would be but always did the right thing. If I was disappointed about something, he would ask only: "Did you do your best?"

Strangely enough, a McKinsey founder, Marvin Bower, stated the same philosophy in a different way. Marvin always believed that if your actions were consistent with the firm's values—of client service, of people development—the financial results would follow in the long run.

MICHAEL D. PARKER *is the president and CEO of Dow Chemical in Midland, Michigan.*

I learned about leadership from experience and from people, especially my mother. She didn't have a lot of education. She faced a lot of difficult and challenging circumstances in her life, and she always met them with calmness and grace. She never panicked.

I played a lot of sports as a kid, and she made sure I never got carried away by the highs and lows of winning and losing. If I won a close tennis match, she would make sure I understood why I won. Maybe she would help me reflect on three crucial points in the match. If I lost, she would help me understand why. We'd talk it over, and eventually I would figure it out. Maybe the sun was in my eyes when I was serving from the right-hand court.

Another thing she would always tell me is that we live in a small community. Your neighbors are right next door, so they're going to *The dumbest questions can* know what kind of people *be very powerful. They* you are whether you like it *can unlock a conversation.* or not. That's a hallmark of Dow to this day: We're a small-town company. We have facilities in places like Freeport, Texas, and Terneuzen, in the Netherlands, and we try to conduct our business in a way that our neighbors can respect and that brings talent and wealth to the community.

A lot of bad leadership, I think, comes from an inability or unwillingness to ask questions. I have watched talented people—people with much higher IQs than mine—who have failed as leaders. They can talk brilliantly, with a great breadth of knowledge, but they're not very good at asking questions. So while they know a lot at a high level, they don't know what's going on way down in the system. Sometimes they are afraid of asking dumb questions, but what they don't realize is that the dumbest questions can be very powerful. They can unlock a conversation.

RICHARD H. BROWN *is the chairman and CEO of EDS in Dallas.*

I trace my leadership philosophy to my mother and father. My father was a math teacher, very bright, with an original mind and an incredible ability to communicate.

He was the decision maker and disciplinarian in the family. My mother was gregarious and affable, and she was always able to find the best in people. She was a terrific motivator and energy supplier. I try to blend the best of both of them by having a disposition that's rooted in realism while keeping my compass pointed on the positive side of human nature.

I'm not crazy about sports metaphors, but I also learned a lot from my baseball coach at Ohio University. At EDS, I'm constantly reminding people to be bold and take chances—incremental changes aren't worth the expenditure of calories. And I got that from my coach. He told us, "If you're going to strike out, strike out swinging. I don't want to catch you looking at a called third strike." I want everybody at EDS to take their best cut at the pitch. People who take a swing move the business forward, even if they strike out once in a while.

Bad leadership happens when leaders put their personal desires ahead of their good judgment. They may know they need to have a tough talk with someone—not mean-spirited, but tough—and they shy away from having that conversation because they want to be well liked, they want to be thought of as nice guys. What they don't understand is that people will accept a tough leader if they believe he's fair. And the most unfair thing you can do to people, I think, is not to tell them candidly how they're doing.

It isn't easy to have these conversations—if it were, we wouldn't need leaders. But I always apply a mental test before I go into one of these talks. I ask myself, "If I were on the receiving end of this message, would I think it was a fair thing to say to me?" You see, people inherently want to do a good job. As long as what you say is well intentioned and constructive—if it helps them improve their performance—people will accept what you have to say, even if it's candid, even if it's kind of hard to swallow.

NOEL M. TICHY *is a professor at the University of Michigan Business School in Ann Arbor. In the 1980s, he ran GE's leadership development center in Crotonville, New York.*

The great academics have, of course, shaped my thinking about leadership: James McGregor Burns, Warren Bennis, and Peter Drucker. But when it comes to deep impact, one year and one place taught me the two most important lessons of leadership I have ever learned: It was 1978 in Hazard, Kentucky.

The Robert Wood Johnson Foundation asked me to head up an effort to transform Hazard Family Health Services from four loosely connected rural health clinics into a community-based, interdisciplinary set of teams of health care providers—nurses, nutritionists, social workers, family health workers. Very innovative. The only problem was, we'd been counting on national health insurance becoming a reality. It didn't. Then the week I arrived, the United Mine Workers cut back their health benefits. Our parent organization, a ten-hospital chain called the Appalachian Regional Hospital System, became insolvent and couldn't meet its payroll, wiping out much of the clinic's budget.

So there I was, running a clinic that had no money. I saw scenes that changed me—nurses weeping over babies who died because we didn't have the resources to save them, staff members completely distraught because they'd been laid off. We were basically putting people into poverty. It was terrible.

But I had to keep the place going; I had to keep morale up. And so I learned to make hard decisions—I call them "edge decisions" now. These are decisions that require the leader to make trade-offs—big ones, the kind that can save an organization or destroy it. I quickly found out that to make edge decisions, you have to have a clear, strong set of values based on the mission of the organization. If you don't measure every decision against those values, you're just shooting from the hip, and that's not leadership. I spent that whole year making edge decisions for the greater good of the clinic, and while people suffered, no one questioned what I was doing or why. That helped keep us going.

The other lesson I learned in Hazard was that the leader is the organization's main source of positive energy. But to play that role, the leader has to have his own sources of emotional energy or he'll be sucked dry. I turned to my family and friends for that, and if I hadn't, I don't know if I would have lasted.

As for negative examples of leadership, I need only think back to early 2000, when I spent a couple of hours with Michael Saylor, the CEO of MicroStrategy. At the time, Saylor was worth $16 billion, and his company was going to rule the world. He was going to build a cyber university, he said, that would put the academy out of business. He blew me away, but at least I had the presence of mind to say, "Hey, maybe this is a bubble." He replied, "The only people who think this is a bubble are the executives at GE and people like you." It was insulting, but still, I walked away thinking, "This guy is going to change things."

Well, he sure fooled me—and a lot of other people besides. A few weeks later, he was accused by regulators of overbooking revenues, and MicroStrategy's big troubles began. Today, the company is a shadow of what it was. When I look back, I'm struck by Saylor's total lack of humility. The hubris was astonishing, and yet we all got seduced by the arrogance. That is not leadership. Leaders listen, and they are hungry to learn; they're sensitive to other people. We can't ever forget that, even when we're being dazzled by someone big and new and successful.

Those are my stories. They remind me of something I tell my students all the time: Leadership is autobiographical. If I don't know your life story, I don't know a thing about you as a leader.

Originally published in December 2001
Reprint R0111B

Primal Leadership

The Hidden Driver of Great Performance

DANIEL GOLEMAN, RICHARD BOYATZIS,
AND ANNIE MCKEE

Executive Summary

YOU'VE HEARD ABOUT THE importance of emotional
intelligence in the workplace—that there's an incontrovertible link between executives' emotional maturity, exemplified by such capabilities as self-awareness and empathy,
and their financial performance. Now, new research
extends that base.

Drawing on two years of research, the authors contend that the leader's mood and his or her attendant
behaviors have enormous effects on bottom line performance. Moods are, quite literally, contagious: A cranky
and ruthless boss creates a toxic organization of negative underachievers; an upbeat and inspirational leader
spawns acolytes for whom any challenge is surmountable. And the final link in the chain is performance: profit
and loss.

Since leaders' moods and behaviors are such potent drivers of business success, top executives' premier job—their primal task, even—is emotional leadership. In other words, before leaders can turn to setting strategy, fixing budgets, or hiring staff, they must first attend to the impact of their moods and behaviors. To help them do that, the authors introduce a five-step process of self-reflection and planning. Executives should ask themselves: Who do I want to be? Who am I now? How do I get from here to there? How do I make change stick? And who can help me? Working through this process will help leaders determine how their emotional leadership is driving the moods and actions of their organizations, and how to adjust their behavior accordingly.

That's not to say, the authors point out, that a leader's actions aren't critical. But the message sent by neurological, psychological, and organizational research is startling in its clarity. Emotional leadership is the spark that ignites a company's performance.

W HEN THE THEORY OF emotional intelligence at work began to receive widespread attention, we frequently heard executives say—in the same breath, mind you—"That's incredible," and, "Well, I've known that all along." They were responding to our research that showed an incontrovertible link between an executive's emotional maturity, exemplified by such capabilities as self-awareness and empathy, and his or her financial performance. Simply put, the research showed that "good guys"—that is, emotionally intelligent men and women—finish first.

We've recently compiled two years of new research that, we suspect, will elicit the same kind of reaction.

People will first exclaim, "No way," then quickly add, "But of course." We found that of all the elements affecting bottom-line performance, the importance of the leader's mood and its attendant behaviors are most surprising. That powerful pair set off a chain reaction: The leader's mood and behaviors drive the moods and behaviors of everyone else. A cranky and ruthless boss creates a toxic organization filled with negative underachievers who ignore opportunities; an inspirational, inclusive leader spawns acolytes for whom any challenge is surmountable. The final link in the chain is performance: profit or loss.

Our observation about the overwhelming impact of the leader's "emotional style," as we call it, is not a wholesale departure from our research into emotional intelligence. It does, however, represent a deeper analysis of our earlier assertion that a leader's emotional intelligence creates a certain culture or work environment. High levels of emotional intelligence, our research showed, create climates in which information sharing, trust, healthy risk-taking, and learning flourish. Low levels of emotional intelligence create climates rife with fear and anxiety. Because tense or terrified employees can be very productive in the short term, their organizations may post good results, but they never last.

Our investigation was designed in part to look at how emotional intelligence drives performance—in particular, at how it travels from the leader through the organization to bottom-line results. "What mechanism," we asked, "binds the chain together?" To answer that question, we turned to the latest neurological and psychological research. We also drew on our work with business leaders, observations by our colleagues of hundreds of leaders, and Hay Group data on the leadership styles of thousands of executives. From this body of research, we discovered that emotional intelligence is carried through an organization like electricity through wires. To be more specific, the leader's mood is quite literally contagious, spreading quickly and inexorably throughout the business.

We'll discuss the science of mood contagion in more depth later, but first let's turn to the key implications of our finding. If a leader's mood and accompanying behaviors are indeed such potent drivers of business success, then a leader's premier task—we would even say his primal task—is emotional leadership. A leader needs to make sure that not only is he regularly in an optimistic, authentic, high-energy mood, but also that, through his chosen actions, his followers feel and act that way, too. Managing for financial results, then, begins with the leader managing his inner life so that the right emotional and behavioral chain reaction occurs.

Managing one's inner life is not easy, of course. For many of us, it's our most difficult challenge. And accurately gauging how one's emotions affect others can be just as difficult. We know of one CEO, for example, who was certain that everyone saw him as upbeat and reliable; his direct reports told us they found his cheerfulness strained, even fake, and his decisions erratic. (We call this common disconnect "CEO disease.") The implication is that primal leadership demands more than putting on a game face every day. It requires an executive to determine, through reflective analysis, how his emotional leadership drives the moods and actions of the organization, and then, with equal discipline, to adjust his behavior accordingly.

That's not to say that leaders can't have a bad day or week: Life happens. And our research doesn't suggest that good moods have to be high-pitched or nonstop—

optimistic, sincere, and realistic will do. But there is no escaping the conclusion that a leader must first attend to the impact of his mood and behaviors before moving on to his wide panoply of other critical responsibilities. In this article, we introduce a process that executives can follow to assess how others experience their leadership, and we discuss ways to calibrate that impact. But first, we'll look at why moods aren't often discussed in the workplace, how the brain works to make moods contagious, and what you need to know about CEO disease.

No Way! Yes Way

When we said earlier that people will likely respond to our new finding by saying "No way," we weren't joking. The fact is, the emotional impact of a leader is almost never discussed in the workplace, let alone in the literature on leadership and performance. For most people, "mood" feels too personal. Even though Americans can be shockingly candid about personal matters—witness the *Jerry Springer Show* and its ilk—we are also the most legally bound. We can't even ask the age of a job applicant. Thus, a conversation about an executive's mood or the moods he creates in his employees might be construed as an invasion of privacy.

We also might avoid talking about a leader's emotional style and its impact because, frankly, the topic feels soft. When was the last time you evaluated a subordinate's mood as part of her performance appraisal? You may have alluded to it—"Your work is hindered by an often negative perspective," or "Your enthusiasm is terrific"—but it is unlikely you mentioned mood outright, let alone discussed its impact on the organization's results.

And yet our research undoubtedly will elicit a "But of course" reaction, too. Everyone knows how much a leader's emotional state drives performance because everyone has had, at one time or another, the inspirational experience of working for an upbeat manager or the crushing experience of toiling for a sour-spirited boss. The former made everything feel possible, and as a result, stretch goals were achieved, competitors beaten, and new customers won. The latter made work grueling. In the shadow of the boss's dark mood, other parts of the organization became "the enemy," colleagues became suspicious of one another, and customers slipped away.

Our research, and research by other social scientists, confirms the verity of these experiences. (There are, of course, rare cases when a brutal boss produces terrific results. We explore that dynamic in "Those Wicked Bosses Who Win" at the end of this article.) The studies are too numerous to mention here but, in aggregate, they show that when the leader is in a happy mood, the people around him view everything in a more positive light. That, in turn, makes them optimistic about achieving their goals, enhances their creativity and the efficiency of their decision making, and predisposes them to be helpful. Research conducted by Alice Isen at Cornell in 1999, for example, found that an upbeat environment fosters mental efficiency, making people better at taking in and understanding information, at using decision rules in complex judgments, and at being flexible in their thinking. Other research directly links mood and financial performance. In 1986, for instance, Martin Seligman and Peter Schulman of the University of Pennsylvania demonstrated that insurance agents who had a "glass half-full" outlook were far more able than their more pessimistic peers to persist despite rejections, and thus, they

closed more sales. (For more information on these studies and a list of our research base, visit www.eiconsor-
tium.org.)

Many leaders whose emotional styles create a dys-
functional environment are eventually fired. (Of course,
that's rarely the stated reason; poor results are.) But it
doesn't have to end that way. Just as a bad mood can be
turned around, so can the spread of toxic feelings from
an emotionally inept leader. A look inside the brain
explains both why and how.

The Science of Moods

A growing body of research on the human brain proves
that, for better or worse, leaders' moods affect the emotions of the people around them. The reason for that lies
in what scientists call the open-loop nature of the brain's
limbic system, our emotional center. A closed-loop system is self-regulating, whereas an open-loop system
depends on external sources to manage itself. In other
words, we rely on connections with other people to
determine our moods. The open-loop limbic system was
a winning design in evolution because it let people come
to one another's emotional rescue—enabling a mother,
for example, to soothe her crying infant.

The open-loop design serves the same purpose today
as it did thousands of years ago. Research in intensive
care units has shown, for example, that the comforting
presence of another person not only lowers the patient's
blood pressure but also slows the secretion of fatty acids
that block arteries. Another study found that three or
more incidents of intense stress within a year (for example, serious financial trouble, being fired, or a divorce)
triples the death rate in socially isolated middle-aged

men, but it has no impact on the death rate of men with many close relationships.

Scientists describe the open loop as "interpersonal limbic regulation"; one person transmits signals that can alter hormone levels, cardiovascular functions, sleep rhythms, even immune functions, inside the body of another. That's how couples are able to trigger surges of oxytocin in each other's brains, creating a pleasant, affectionate feeling. But in all aspects of social life, our physiologies intermingle. Our limbic system's open-loop design lets other people change our very physiology and hence, our emotions.

Even though the open loop is so much a part of our lives, we usually don't notice the process. Scientists have captured the attunement of emotions in the laboratory by measuring the physiology—such as heart rate—of two people sharing a good conversation. As the interaction begins, their bodies operate at different rhythms. But after 15 minutes, the physiological profiles of their bodies look remarkably similar.

Researchers have seen again and again how emotions spread irresistibly in this way whenever people are near one another. As far back as 1981, psychologists Howard Friedman and Ronald Riggio found that even completely nonverbal expressiveness can affect other people. For example, when three strangers sit facing one another in silence for a minute or two, the most emotionally expressive of the three transmits his or her mood to the other two—without a single word being spoken.

The same holds true in the office, boardroom, or shop floor; group members inevitably "catch" feelings from one another. In 2000, Caroline Bartel at New York University and Richard Saavedra at the University of Michigan found that in 70 work teams across diverse industries, people in meetings together ended up sharing moods —both good and bad—within two hours. One study asked teams of nurses and accountants to monitor their moods over weeks; researchers discovered that their emotions tracked together, and they were largely independent of each team's shared hassles. Groups, therefore, like individuals, ride emotional roller coasters, sharing everything from jealousy to angst to euphoria. (A good mood, incidentally, spreads most swiftly by the judicious use of humor. For more on this, see "Smile and the World Smiles with You" at the end of this article.)

Moods that start at the top tend to move the fastest because everyone watches the boss. They take their emotional cues from him. Even when the boss isn't highly visible—for example, the CEO who works behind closed doors on an upper floor—his attitude affects the moods of his direct reports, and a domino effect ripples throughout the company.

Call That CEO a Doctor

If the leader's mood is so important, then he or she had better get into a good one, right? Yes, but the full answer is more complicated than that. A leader's mood has the greatest impact on performance when it is upbeat. But it must also be in tune with those around him. We call this dynamic *resonance*. (For more on this, see "Get Happy, Carefully" at the end of this article.)

We found that an alarming number of leaders do not really know if they have resonance with their organizations. Rather, they suffer from CEO disease; its one unpleasant symptom is the sufferer's near-total ignorance about how his mood and actions appear to the organization. It's not that leaders don't care how they are perceived; most do. But they incorrectly assume that they can decipher this information themselves. Worse, they think that if they are having a negative effect, someone will tell them. They're wrong.

As one CEO in our research explains, "I so often feel I'm not getting the truth. I can never put my finger on it, because no one is actually lying to me. But I can sense that people are hiding information or camouflaging key facts. They aren't lying, but neither are they telling me everything I need to know. I'm always second-guessing."

People don't tell leaders the whole truth about their emotional impact for many reasons. Sometimes they are scared of being the bearer of bad news—and getting shot. Others feel it isn't their place to comment on such a personal topic. Still others don't realize that what they really want to talk about is the effects of the leader's emotional style—that feels too vague. Whatever the reason, the CEO can't rely on his followers to spontaneously give him the full picture.

Taking Stock

The process we recommend for self-discovery and personal reinvention is neither newfangled nor born of pop psychology, like so many self-help programs offered to executives today. Rather, it is based on three streams of research into how executives can improve the emotional intelligence capabilities most closely linked to effective leadership. (Information on these research streams can also be found at www.eiconsortium.org.) In 1989, one of us (Richard Boyatzis) began drawing on this body of research to design the five-step process itself, and since then, thousands of executives have used it successfully.

Unlike more traditional forms of coaching, our process is based on brain science. A person's emotional skills—the attitude and abilities with which someone approaches life and work—are not genetically hardwired, like eye color and skin tone. But in some ways they might as well be, because they are so deeply embedded in our neurology.

A person's emotional skills do, in fact, have a genetic component. Scientists have discovered, for instance, the gene for shyness—which is not a mood, per se, but it can certainly drive a person toward a persistently quiet demeanor, which may be read as a "down" mood. Other people are preternaturally jolly—that is, their relentless cheerfulness seems preternatural until you meet their peppy parents. As one executive explains, "All I know is that ever since I was a baby, I have always been happy. It drives some people crazy, but I couldn't get blue if I tried. And my brother is the exact same way; he saw the bright side of life, even during his divorce."

Even though emotional skills are partly inborn, experience plays a major role in how the genes are expressed. A happy baby whose parents die or who endures physical abuse may grow into a melancholy adult. A cranky toddler may turn into a cheerful adult after discovering a fulfilling avocation. Still, research suggests that our range of emotional skills is relatively set by our mid-20s and that our accompanying behaviors are, by that time, deep-seated habits. And therein lies the rub: The more we act a certain way—be it happy, depressed, or cranky—the more the behavior becomes ingrained in our brain circuitry, and the more we will continue to feel and act that way.

That's why emotional intelligence matters so much for a leader. An emotionally intelligent leader can monitor his or her moods through self-awareness, change them for the better through self-management, understand their impact through empathy, and act in ways that boost others' moods through relationship management.

The following five-part process is designed to rewire the brain toward more emotionally intelligent behaviors. The process begins with imagining your ideal self and then coming to terms with your real self, as others experience you. The next step is creating a tactical plan to bridge the gap between ideal and real, and after that, to practice those activities. It concludes with creating a community of colleagues and family—call them change enforcers—to keep the process alive. Let's look at the steps in more detail.

"WHO DO I WANT TO BE?"

Sofia, a senior manager at a northern European telecommunications company, knew she needed to understand how her emotional leadership affected others. Whenever she felt stressed, she tended to communicate poorly and take over subordinates' work so that the job would be done "right." Attending leadership seminars hadn't changed her habits, and neither had reading management books or working with mentors.

When Sofia came to us, we asked her to imagine herself eight years from now as an effective leader and to write a description of a typical day. "What would she be doing?" we asked. "Where would she live? Who would be there? How would it feel?" We urged her to consider her deepest values and loftiest dreams and to explain how those ideals had become a part of her everyday life.

Sofia pictured herself leading her own tight-knit company staffed by ten colleagues. She was enjoying an open relationship with her daughter and had trusting relationships with her friends and coworkers. She saw herself as a relaxed and happy leader and parent and as loving and empowering to all those around her.

In general, Sofia had a low level of self-awareness: She was rarely able to pinpoint why she was struggling at work and at home. All she could say was, "Nothing is working right." This exercise, which prompted her to picture what life would look life if everything were going right, opened her eyes to the missing elements in her emotional style. She was able to see the impact she had on people in her life.

"WHO AM I NOW?"

In the next step of the discovery process, you come to see your leadership style as others do. This is both difficult and dangerous. Difficult, because few people have the guts to tell the boss or a colleague what he's really like. And dangerous, because such information can sting or even paralyze. A small bit of ignorance about yourself isn't always a bad thing: Ego-defense mechanisms have their advantages. Research by Martin Seligman shows that high-functioning people generally feel more optimistic about their prospects and possibilities than average performers. Their rose-colored lenses, in fact, fuel the enthusiasm and energy that make the unexpected and the extraordinary achievable. Playwright Henrik Ibsen called such self-delusions "vital lies," soothing mistruths we let ourselves believe in order to face a daunting world.

But self-delusion should come in very small doses. Executives should relentlessly seek the truth about themselves, especially since it is sure to be somewhat diluted when they hear it anyway. One way to get the truth is to keep an extremely open attitude toward critiques. Another is to seek out negative feedback, even cultivating a colleague or two to play devil's advocate.

We also highly recommend gathering feedback from as many people as possible—including bosses, peers, and subordinates. Feedback from subordinates and peers is especially helpful because it most accurately predicts a leader's effectiveness, two, four, and even seven years out, according to research by Glenn McEvoy at Utah State and Richard Beatty at Rutgers University.

Of course, 360-degree feedback doesn't specifically ask people to evaluate your moods, actions, and their impact. But it does reveal how people experience you. For instance, when people rate how well you listen, they are really reporting how well they think you hear them. Similarly, when 360-degree feedback elicits ratings about coaching effectiveness, the answers show whether or not people feel you understand and care about them. When the feedback uncovers low scores on, say, openness to new ideas, it means that people experience you as inaccessible or unapproachable or both. In sum, all you need to know about your emotional impact is in 360-degree feedback, if you look for it.

One last note on this second step. It is, of course, crucial to identify your areas of weakness. But focusing only on your weaknesses can be dispiriting. That's why it is just as important, maybe even more so, to understand your strengths. Knowing where your real self overlaps with your ideal self will give you the positive energy you need to move forward to the next step in the process—bridging the gaps.

"HOW DO I GET FROM HERE TO THERE?"

Once you know who you want to be and have compared it with how people see you, you need to devise an action plan. For Sofia, this meant planning for a real improvement in her level of self-awareness. So she asked each member of her team at work to give her feedback—weekly, anonymously, and in written form—about her mood and performance and their affect on people. She also committed herself to three tough but achievable tasks: spending an hour each day reflecting on her behavior in a journal, taking a class on group dynamics at a local college, and enlisting the help of a trusted colleague as an informal coach.

Consider, too, how Juan, a marketing executive for the Latin American division of a major integrated energy company, completed this step. Juan was charged with growing the company in his home country of Venezuela as well as in the entire region—a job that would require him to be a coach and a visionary and to have an encouraging, optimistic outlook. Yet 360-degree feedback revealed that Juan was seen as intimidating and internally focused. Many of his direct reports saw him as a grouch—impossible to please at his worst, and emotionally draining at his best.

Identifying this gap allowed Juan to craft a plan with manageable steps toward improvement. He knew he needed to hone his powers of empathy if he wanted to develop a coaching style, so he committed to various activities that would let him practice that skill. For instance, Juan decided to get to know each of his subordinates better; if he understood more about who they were, he thought, he'd be more able to help them reach their goals. He made plans with each employee to meet outside of work, where they might be more comfortable revealing their feelings.

Juan also looked for areas outside of his job to forge his missing links—for example, coaching his daughter's soccer team and volunteering at a local crisis center.

Both activities helped him to experiment with how well he understood others and to try out new behaviors.

Again, let's look at the brain science at work. Juan was trying to overcome ingrained behaviors—his approach to work had taken hold over time, without his realizing it. Bringing them into awareness was a crucial step toward changing them. As he paid more attention, the situations that arose—while listening to a colleague, coaching soccer, or talking on the phone to someone who was distraught—all became cues that stimulated him to break old habits and try new responses.

This cueing for habit change is neural as well as perceptual. Researchers at the University of Pittsburgh and Carnegie Mellon University have shown that as we mentally prepare for a task, we activate the prefrontal cortex—the part of the brain that moves us into action. The greater the prior activation, the better we do at the task.

Such mental preparation becomes particularly important when we're trying to replace an old habit with a better one. As neuroscientist Cameron Carter at the University of Pittsburgh found, the prefrontal cortex becomes particularly active when a person prepares to overcome a habitual response. The aroused prefrontal cortex marks the brain's focus on what's about to happen. Without that arousal, a person will reenact tried-and-true but undesirable routines: The executive who just doesn't listen will once again cut off his subordinate, a ruthless leader will launch into yet another critical attack, and so on. That's why a learning agenda is so important. Without one, we literally do not have the brainpower to change.

"HOW DO I MAKE CHANGE STICK?"

In short, making change last requires practice. The reason, again, lies in the brain. It takes doing and redoing, over and over, to break old neural habits. A leader must rehearse a new behavior until it becomes automatic— that is, until he's mastered it at the level of implicit learning. Only then will the new wiring replace the old.

While it is best to practice new behaviors, as Juan did, sometimes just envisioning them will do. Take the case of Tom, an executive who wanted to close the gap between his real self (perceived by colleagues and subordinates to be cold and hard driving) and his ideal self (a visionary and a coach).

Tom's learning plan involved finding opportunities to step back and coach his employees rather than jumping down their throats when he sensed they were wrong. Tom also began to spend idle moments during his commute thinking through how to handle encounters he would have that day. One morning, while en route to a breakfast meeting with an employee who seemed to be bungling a project, Tom ran through a positive scenario in his mind. He asked questions and listened to be sure he fully understood the situation before trying to solve the problem. He anticipated feeling impatient, and he rehearsed how he would handle these feelings.

Studies on the brain affirm the benefits of Tom's visualization technique: Imagining something in vivid detail can fire the same brain cells actually involved in doing that activity. The new brain circuitry appears to go through its paces, strengthening connections, even when we merely repeat the sequence in our minds. So to alleviate the fears associated with trying out riskier ways of leading, we should first visualize some likely scenarios. Doing so will make us feel less awkward when we actually put the new skills into practice.

Experimenting with new behaviors and seizing opportunities inside and outside of work to practice them—as well as using such methods as mental rehearsal—eventually triggers in our brains the neural connections necessary for genuine change to occur. Even so, lasting change doesn't happen through experimentation and brainpower alone. We need, as the song goes, a little help from our friends.

"WHO CAN HELP ME?"

The fifth step in the self-discovery and reinvention process is creating a community of supporters. Take, for example, managers at Unilever who formed learning groups as part of their executive development process. At first, they gathered to discuss their careers and how to provide leadership. But because they were also charged with discussing their dreams and their learning goals, they soon realized that they were discussing both their work and their personal lives. They developed a strong mutual trust and began relying on one another for frank feedback as they worked on strengthening their leadership abilities. When this happens, the business benefits through stronger performance. Many professionals today have created similar groups, and for good reason. People we trust let us try out unfamiliar parts of our leadership repertoire without risk.

We cannot improve our emotional intelligence or change our leadership style without help from others. We not only practice with other people but also rely on them to create a safe environment in which to experiment. We need to get feedback about how our actions affect others and to assess our progress on our learning agenda.

In fact, perhaps paradoxically, in the self-directed learning process we draw on others every step of the way—from articulating and refining our ideal self and comparing it with the reality to the final assessment that affirms our progress. Our relationships offer us the very context in which we understand our progress and comprehend the usefulness of what we're learning.

Mood over Matter

When we say that managing your mood and the moods of your followers is the task of primal leadership, we certainly don't mean to suggest that mood is all that matters. As we've noted, your actions are critical, and mood and actions together must resonate with the organization and with reality. Similarly, we acknowledge all the other challenges leaders must conquer—from strategy to hiring to new product development. It's all in a long day's work.

But taken as a whole, the message sent by neurological, psychological, and organizational research is startling in its clarity. Emotional leadership is the spark that ignites a company's performance, creating a bonfire of success or a landscape of ashes. Moods matter that much.

Those Wicked Bosses Who Win

EVERYONE KNOWS OF A RUDE and coercive CEO who, by all appearances, epitomizes the antithesis of emotional intelligence yet seems to reap great business results. If a leader's mood matters so much, how can we explain those mean-spirited, successful SOBs?

First, let's take a closer look at them. Just because a particular executive is the most visible, he may not actually lead the company. A CEO who heads a conglomerate may have no followers to speak of; it's his division heads who actively lead people and affect profitability.

Second, sometimes an SOB leader has strengths that counterbalance his caustic behavior, but they don't attract as much attention in the business press. In his early days at GE, Jack Welch exhibited a strong hand at the helm as he undertook a radical company turnaround. At that time and in that situation, Welch's firm, top-down style was appropriate. What got less press was how Welch subsequently settled into a more emotionally intelligent leadership style, especially when he articulated a new vision for the company and mobilized people to follow it.

Those caveats aside, let's get back to those infamous corporate leaders who seem to have achieved sterling business results despite their brutish approaches to leadership. Skeptics cite Bill Gates, for example, as a leader who gets away with a harsh style that should theoretically damage his company.

But our leadership model, which shows the effectiveness of specific leadership styles in specific situations, puts Gates's supposedly negative behaviors in a different light. (Our model is explained in detail in the HBR article "Leadership That Gets Results," which appeared in the March–April 2000 issue.) Gates is the achievement-driven leader par excellence, in an organization that has cherry-picked highly talented and motivated people. His apparently harsh leadership style—baldly challenging employees to surpass their past performance—can be quite effective when employees are competent, motivated, and need little direction—all characteristics of Microsoft's engineers.

In short, it's all too easy for a skeptic to argue against the importance of leaders who manage their moods by citing a "rough and tough" leader who achieved good business results despite his bad behavior. We contend that there are, of course, exceptions to the rule, and that in some specific business cases, an SOB boss resonates just fine. But in general, leaders who are jerks must reform or else their moods and actions will eventually catch up with them.

Smile and the World Smiles with You

REMEMBER THAT OLD CLICHÉ? It's not too far from the truth. As we've shown, mood contagion is a real neurological phenomenon, but not all emotions spread with the same ease. A 1999 study conducted by Sigal Barsade at the Yale School of Management showed that, among working groups, cheerfulness and warmth spread easily, while irritability caught on less so, and depression least of all.

It should come as no surprise that laughter is the most contagious of all emotions. Hearing laughter, we find it almost impossible not to laugh or smile, too. That's because some of our brain's open-loop circuits are designed to detect smiles and laughter, making us respond in kind. Scientists theorize that this dynamic was hardwired into our brains ages ago because smiles and laughter had a way of cementing alliances, thus helping the species survive.

The main implication here for leaders undertaking the primal task of managing their moods and the moods of others is this: Humor hastens the spread of an upbeat climate. But like the leader's mood in general, humor must resonate with the organization's culture and its reality. Smiles and laughter, we would posit, are only contagious when they're genuine.

Get Happy, Carefully

GOOD MOODS GALVANIZE good performance, but it doesn't make sense for a leader to be as chipper as a blue jay at dawn if sales are tanking or the business is going under. The most effective executives display moods and behaviors that match the situation at hand, with a healthy dose of optimism mixed in. They respect how other people are feeling—even if it is glum or defeated—but they also model what it looks like to move forward with hope and humor.

This kind of performance, which we call resonance, is for all intents and purposes the four components of emotional intelligence in action.

Self-awareness, perhaps the most essential of the emotional intelligence competencies, is the ability to read your own emotions. It allows people to know their strengths and limitations and feel confident about their self-worth. Resonant leaders use self-awareness to gauge their own moods accurately, and they intuitively know how they are affecting others.

Self-management is the ability to control your emotions and act with honesty and integrity In reliable and adaptable ways. Resonant leaders don't let their occasional bad moods seize the day; they use self-management to leave it outside the office or to explain its source to people in a reasonable manner, so they know where it's coming from and how long it might last.

Social awareness includes the key capabilities of empathy and organizational intuition. Socially aware executives do more than sense other people's emotions, they show that they care. Further, they are experts at reading the currents of office politics. Thus, resonant leaders often keenly understand how their words and actions make others feel, and they are sensitive enough to change them when that impact is negative.

Relationship management, the last of the emotional intelligence competencies, includes the abilities to communicate clearly and convincingly, disarm conflicts, and build strong personal bonds. Resonant leaders use these skills to spread their enthusiasm and solve disagreements, often with humor and kindness.

As effective as resonant leadership is, it is just as rare. Most people suffer through dissonant leaders whose toxic moods and upsetting behaviors wreck havoc before a hopeful and realistic leader repairs the situation.

Consider what happened recently at an experimental division of the BBC, the British media giant. Even though the group's 200 or so journalists and editors had given their best effort, management decided to close the division.

The shutdown itself was bad enough, but the brusque, contentious mood and manner of the executive sent to deliver the news to the assembled staff incited something beyond the expected frustration. People became enraged—at both the decision and the bearer of the news. The executive's cranky mood and delivery created an atmosphere so threatening that he had to call security to be ushered from the room.

The next day, another executive visited the same staff. His mood was somber and respectful, as was his behavior. He spoke about the importance of journalism to the vibrancy of a society and of the calling that had drawn them all to the field in the first place. He reminded them that no one goes into journalism to get rich—as a profession its finances have always been marginal, job security ebbing and flowing with the larger economic tides. He recalled a time in his own career when he had been let go and how he had struggled to find a new position—but how he had stayed dedicated to the profession. Finally, he wished them well in getting on with their careers.

The reaction from what had been an angry mob the day before? When this resonant leader finished speaking, the staff cheered.

Resonance in Times of Crisis

WHEN TALKING ABOUT LEADERS' moods, the importance of resonance cannot be overstated. While our research suggests that leaders should generally be upbeat, their behavior must be rooted in realism, especially when faced with a crisis.

Consider the response of Bob Mulholland, senior VP and head of the client relations group at Merrill Lynch, to the terrorist attacks in New York. On September 11, 2001, Mulholland and his staff in Two World Financial Center felt the building rock, then watched as smoke poured out of a gaping hole in the building directly across from theirs. People started panicking: Some ran frantically from window to window. Others were paralyzed with fear. Those with relatives working in the World Trade Center were terrified for their safety. Mulholland knew he had to act: "When there's a crisis, you've got to show people the way, step by step, and make sure you're taking care of their concerns."

He started by getting people the information they needed to "unfreeze." He found out, for instance, which floors employees' relatives worked on and assured them that they'd have enough time to escape. Then he calmed the panic-stricken, one at a time. "We're getting out of here now," he said quietly, "and you're coming with me. Not the elevator, take the stairs." He remained calm and decisive, yet he didn't minimize people's emotional responses. Thanks to him, everyone escaped before the towers collapsed.

Mulholland's leadership didn't end there. Recognizing that this event would touch each client personally, he and his team devised a way for financial consultants to connect with their clients on an emotional level. They called every client to ask, "How are you? Are your loved ones okay? How are you feeling?" As Mulholland explains, "There was no way to pick up and do business as usual. The first order of 'business' was letting our clients know we really do care."

Bob Mulholland courageously performed one of the most crucial emotional tasks of leadership: He helped himself and his people find meaning in the face of chaos and madness. To do so, he first attuned to and expressed the shared emotional reality. That's why the direction he eventually articulated resonated at the gut level. His words and his actions reflected what people were feeling in their hearts.

Originally published in December 2001
Reprint R0111C

All in a Day's Work

MODERATED BY HARRIS COLLINGWOOD

AND JULIA KIRBY

Executive Summary

EXECUTIVES ARE BUSY PEOPLE. They have too much to do and certainly too much to read. Yet judging from the books and magazines they buy, executives are never too time-pressed or information-saturated to learn more about leadership. The hunger for knowledge about leadership is not simply a reaction to the twists and turns in the business cycle. It's a desire to beef up scarce resources: Just as no baseball team has ever had too many good pitchers, business has never suffered from a glut of true leaders. Ask any follower.

In this roundtable, six experts from the corporate world, the nonprofit sector, and academia tackle tough questions about leadership. Can leadership be taught? What do good leaders do, and what do they do better than most? The discussion, which took place at the New York Stock Exchange's headquarters in Manhattan in

August 2001, began with what leaders ought to do. The emphasis differed from one person to the next, but comments touched on three common themes: the need to formulate and communicate a vision for an organization; the need for a leader to add value to an enterprise; and an organizational imperative for a leader to motivate followers.

Conversation then turned to how leaders ought to lead, focusing on topics such as the leadership role of the generalist in organizations and the need to remain calm and decisive in a crisis. Reflecting their widely varying backgrounds, the participants drew on their experiences in the business world, the military, evolutionary anthropology, and psychotherapy to help them drive home their views on developing new leaders, rewarding extraordinary effort, and keeping organizations focused on their missions.

Listen in.

Executives are busy people. They have too much to do and certainly too much to read. Yet judging from the books and magazines they buy and the conferences they attend, executives are never too time-pressed or information-saturated to learn more about leadership.

The reasons aren't hard to find. If the need for vigorous, effective leadership was great when the potential of the technological revolution seemed limitless and the risk negligible, how much more urgent is that need now that the national mood has darkened and our confidence in a prosperous and secure future has been dreadfully shaken? But the hunger for knowledge about leadership predates the atrocities of September 11. Whether the times are good or bad, business has never suffered from a leadership glut. Ask any follower.

There is far more interest in leadership, however, than there is agreement on it. No topic in business is more hotly debated. Can leadership be taught? Are its skills portable? What makes a leader, anyway? More to the point, what are the most important tasks of a good leader? How do the most effective leaders invest their time? In short, what do good leaders do, and what do they do better than most? HBR senior editors Harris Collingwood and Julia Kirby sat down in August 2001 with six leaders and leadership experts from the corporate world, the nonprofit sector, and academia (see the list of participants at the end of this article.) to tackle these questions. The discussion, which took place at the New York Stock Exchange's headquarters, began with a consensus on what leaders ought to do. But when the conversation turned to *how* leaders do what they do, opinions began to diverge. Listen in.

HBR: *Several weeks ago, we asked each of you to prepare a list of the three most important tasks of a leader. Let's begin our discussion by reviewing your lists and expanding on what you've written.*

Cynthia Tragge-Lakra: The first thing a leader has to do is set the vision for the organization. That's often said, but it's actually a lot harder to do than you might think. It only comes after hard thought about the capabilities of the organization and the needs of the market. The second task is to understand the changing needs of customers and employees. I've seen a lot of leaders tripped up by their inability to be flexible and adaptable, not just when the marketplace changes but also when employees change. And finally, leaders need to have people follow them. They need to energize people so that they rally behind the vision and take leadership roles themselves in bringing that vision to life.

Raymond Gilmartin: I've got a variation on Cynthia's list. I think an effective leader sees what needs to be done, gets it done, and gets it done in the right way. Seeing what needs to be done basically means that the leader has a conceptual, strategic ability to sense what's going on in the outside world as well as inside the organization. Getting it done means understanding how organizations work in terms of process as well as structure. It also means being able to choose the right people to do the job and then motivating them to do it. And getting it done in the right way means having certain personal qualities. To have a healthy organization, you need leaders who conduct themselves ethically and treat people with dignity and respect.

Abraham Zaleznik: Agreed—leaders do have to have a sense of direction, substantively, for the business. That requires taking a good long time to think about the world and understand where it's moving before your competitors do. I would say, though, that the second thing a leader needs is focus, which is what enables you to drive in a single-minded way in the direction you've decided to go. It also means being highly focused in your relations with other people, whether they're your employees or your customers or your shareholders or the people in the community where you work.

The third task of the leader is what I call identification. This is a little more complicated. I think the job of a leader is to get people to identify with him or her so that the leader becomes a presence in their minds and in their thinking. It sounds pejorative to call it narcissism, but that's what it is. Leaders need to be so aware of themselves and so comfortable with the power they possess that they're willing to let people use them as objects of identification—as totems, almost. This creates enormous cohesion in the organization.

Frances Hesselbein: Everyone so far has focused on what leaders do, and I don't think I would disagree with what's been said. But before we begin to think about what the leader does, perhaps we should think about who the leader is, because a leader defines leadership in his or her own terms. In the end, it's the quality and character of the leader that determines an organization's performance and results. Think about this in relation to the job of transmitting the organization's values. It's not enough for the leader just to say, "These are our values." If those values are really going to permeate the organization, the leader has to embody them. The army has a wonderful shorthand. They say, "Be, know, do." I believe that any discussion of leadership has to begin with how to be.

Frederick Smith: I'm glad Frances mentioned values, because that's where my list begins and ends. The primary task of leadership is to communicate the vision and the values of an organization. Second, leaders must win support for the vision and the values they articulate. And third, leaders have to reinforce the vision and the values. That's probably the most difficult task, and it's where most organizations fall apart. When people say an organization failed because of a lack of leadership, they usually mean its leaders were unable to reinforce the types of activities that lead to success and quit doing the things that don't.

Lionel Tiger: When it comes to the matter of the leader's role, I seem to have gone in a somewhat different direction than the others around the table. A leader's first task, I think, is to have a sense of the inexorability of tomorrow. Today is a wasted resource, as it were. That orientation toward tomorrow is partly a characteristic of *Homo sapiens*, who have big brains and can think of the future in a way that's very direct and very demanding. It's a difficult trick, and not everyone has the brainpower or eyesight—in a metaphorical sense—to pull it off.

Next, a leader should understand probabilities and variation. That is, you have to be able to evaluate quickly and sensibly the odds of accomplishing something. You also have to be able to look analytically at your own organization and appreciate that its activities fall within a normal curve—at one end you have dramatic events, at the other end are mundane events, and the great piece in the middle constitutes normal life.

Finally, and this sounds more obvious than it really is, you can't be a leader without followers, as Cynthia said. The fact is, all primate groups create—cannot exist without—leaders. If there isn't one, there's a period of immense tension and uncertainty, and work doesn't get done. Decisions about the wider set of environmental influences don't get made. All of the group's energy is spent on internal jockeying for dominance.

HBR: *The emphasis differs from one person to the next, but each list seems to touch in one way or another on three common themes. The first would be the necessity of formulating and communicating a vision for the organization. Then comes the need for a leader to add value to the enterprise. And the final theme is the organizational imperative to motivate followers. Let's take up each theme in turn, beginning with vision.*

Gilmartin: I arrived at Merck in 1994 after five years as CEO of Becton-Dickinson. My first order of business was to understand the competitive, regulatory, and scientific environment that Merck operated in and what unique strengths the company brought to that environment. I had a lot to learn, but I pretty quickly came up with the idea that all the information and knowledge I needed were already in the organization. So I undertook a very specific, methodical process of asking a few questions of about 35 to 40 key people in the company. What are the major issues facing us? If you were in my position, where would you focus your time?

What emerged from this process was a vision of what we wanted to do. We want to grow faster than anybody else in our industry, and we want to get there by translating cutting-edge science into breakthrough medicines. These aren't just buzzwords. Cutting-edge science means our scientists work on a disease only when there's new knowledge about its mechanism of action. With that novel understanding, they try to develop drugs that act on that mechanism. And this vision has produced results: a breakthrough drug for osteoporosis, a breakthrough drug for asthma.

Smith: Right—the reason you get results is that a vision gives you a focal point. Other things coalesce around it. For example, when everyone knows the vision, it becomes much easier to have a hard conversation with someone. Those of us here from the corporate world all work for high-performance organizations, and everyone who works at these companies knows the value we place on performance and accountability. That's part of a vision that has been communicated carefully, thoroughly, and frequently. So if an employee's performance slips, if he's not producing, it's not going to come as a surprise when you call him into your office for a tough conversation. That's one big thing a vision does for an organization. It tells people what's expected of them. And that makes it a lot easier to tell them when they're not meeting expectations. You can discuss their conduct and their performance in terms of the vision.

Hesselbein: Vision also keeps you alert. Lionel mentioned that a leader has to have a sense of the future. If we are responsible leaders, we're constantly scanning the environment for changes and for hints of how it will change in the future. This is why, for example, leaders need to pay close attention to rapidly changing demographics. Who are your customers of the future? How you answer that is going to have a major influence on the vision and the mission of your organization. It certainly had an influence on the Girl Scouts. We looked at the changing makeup of the U.S. population, and we looked at our board and our membership and our visual materials, and we asked, "When a young girl looks at our organization, can she find herself?" Making sure that she could find herself wherever she looked became part of our vision, and as a result we tripled racial-minority membership at every level in the organization, including the board, the staff, and the field.

Gilmartin: I think both Fred and Frances are talking about the way that a vision provides a framework through which you view everything that goes on in the company and in the external environment. You have to be disciplined about your activities and your dealings with other people. Everything you do is for a reason, and that reason is contained within the vision.

Merck's vision also determines the way we look at the world outside our company. For instance, we know that for the U.S. drug industry to innovate successfully over the long term, a number of enabling conditions need to be in place. One is that the United States must continue to invest in biomedical research. Another is that we have to have intellectual property protection. And another is that we need access to global markets through free trade. So we're very active in Washington and around the world, trying to shape the external environment in a way that allows us to pursue our vision.

HBR: *Along with formulating a vision, leaders need followers to help them pursue it. But to win the respect and allegiance of followers, it sounds as if leaders need to add value to the organization—and to be seen adding value. So how do you do that, especially if your skills aren't the skills the organization is known for?*

Gilmartin: Since I'm an engineer with an MBA working for a company that's strong on science, maybe I should try to answer that first. There is a big difference between scientists and engineers. When I joined Merck, it was very important for me to be able to quickly establish my credentials as someone who understood science and was aware of its central place in the company. I made a point of becoming engaged in some of the details of the scientific activity and showed real respect and interest. And that got noticed. Our head of research, Ed Scolnick, is someone who says very directly what he's thinking. The other day he said to me, "You know, when you first got here, you were more of an orchestrator, but now you're really adding value."

So apparently I'm adding something that the scientists couldn't do on their own. I'm not sitting there trying to figure out whether or not a scientist is interpreting the data correctly. I let Ed worry about that. But I am able to understand the significance of the science at another level. How does it fit into the overall vision of the company? I also watch the interaction of the scientists. What are the organizational implications of their inter-action? Who are the leaders? How does their work affect the manufacturing side of the business? This comes back to that question of focus: You have to see people and events in the context of the vision.

Zaleznik: Leaders make a mistake if they undervalue the kind of contribution you're talking about. Businesses today are in large part collections of specialists. Yet there's an important leadership role for generalists in these organizations. Generalists can take conceptual leaps across disciplines and make connections that spe-cialists can't see.

Admiral Hyman Rickover, who is known as the father of the nuclear navy, is an example of the creative contri-bution a generalist can make. He was an engineer, not a nuclear physicist. Physicists, and scientists in general, want to investigate why things happen in a particular way. But engineers see the world through a different lens—they want to make things that haven't been made before, or make them better. Rickover understood the sci-ence, but he asked different questions than the scientists. He saw nuclear power as a variable in an engineering problem. That sounds simple, but that shift in perspective had enormous consequences. Because he was able to lead people to a new way of thinking, the navy's nuclear tech-nicians shifted their efforts and energy from doing experi-ments in the lab to building prototypes. It took a whole new mind-set to build these nuclear subs, and it took an extraordinary leader to change the mind-set.

Tragge-Lakra: The term "generalist" is something of a misnomer in this context, though. In my experience,

the best generalists are specialists in some area.
Whether their specialty is marketing or finance, they
have a depth of understanding in a particular discipline
that they're able to bring to bear. Rickover knew something about nuclear physics, but he knew a lot more
about engineering.

Similarly, when you joined Merck, Ray, you had a lot
to learn about organic chemistry, but you already knew a
fair amount about managed care. My guess is you
learned enough about organic chemistry to get a handle
on what the organization was doing, but you didn't try to
interfere with the scientists. People who are new to leadership sometimes need to be reminded that they'll never
be specialists in everything and that they need to rely on
specialists to keep the organization moving forward.

Gilmartin: I don't need to know as much science as
the scientists. I can add value by staying focused—and
reminding everyone else to stay focused—on the purpose
of all our research. That, in short form, is really the job of
the leader.

Smith: Maybe I'm being simplistic, but it seems to
me that the way leaders add value is through leadership.
They're able to get people to coalesce around organizational rather than individual goals. And if they're good
leaders, they motivate people to do their jobs to the best
of their abilities and not just the bare minimum to avoid
getting fired. There are all kinds of ways to encourage
that effort and reinforce it, but the primary tool in the
commercial world is to share the rewards. Whatever system you set up to share the rewards—profit sharing,
management incentive compensation, unexpected
rewards, promotions—isn't as important as what you're
rewarding. The point is to constantly reinforce the organization's vision and values. We have something called

the Golden Falcon Award, which is a pin and a good-sized check we give to employees who go above and beyond for customers. One recipient was a courier in Buffalo, New York, by the name of Joe Kinder, who was supposed to deliver visas to a couple who were going to Russia to adopt a little boy. They needed the visas right away because the Russian government, in literally a matter of days, was going to close the window on all new adoptions by foreigners. Well, the package was misaddressed, and time was growing short, so this courier, on his own initiative, tracked down the package, corrected the address, and then went miles out of his way to hand-deliver the visas. That's the sort of effort you want to recognize and reward and reinforce.

And that's something you can track, by the way. At FedEx, we measure how motivated employees are, and we measure how well they're fulfilling the vision of delivering superior service to our customers. As for motivation, we have been surveying our employees continuously for a quarter of a century. As for the quality of our service, we have a detailed system for measuring that. We put both metrics together to produce what we call the service quality index, or SQI, which is a numerical measurement of service as seen from the customer's point of view, not from ours.

What we're really measuring is leadership. If our employees are happy and our customers are happy, those are signs that the company's leadership is communicating the vision and the values correctly and is rewarding them appropriately. That's a great competitive advantage in a service business like FedEx, where the value chain is outside the four walls. Inside a factory, you can have a six-sigma program or other quality controls to ensure that your product satisfies your customers' needs.

A measure like SQI is the equivalent in a service business. It's really your leadership quotient. If you're looking for the value a good leader can add, that's where you'll find it.

HBR: *Let's tilt the conversation toward the task of energizing followers and developing new leaders. Lionel, could you talk a little about motivation? People talk about it sometimes as if motivation were something leaders did to followers. But isn't it more of an interaction?*

Tiger: Absolutely. Leaders often forget that people arrive on the scene predisposed to do a good job. I'm always impressed with the films—they are invariably terrible films—in which the young player rushes up and says, "Send me in, Coach." People are hardwired to want to be sent in. One of the things good leaders do is allow people to do what is built into them to do anyway, which is to contribute. As opposed to saying to the kid who wants to be sent in, "Sure, sure, send me a memo on that, will you?"

Gilmartin: That's right. People really do want to do a good job. A couple of months ago, I was in one of our manufacturing plants talking to a production operator in charge of a new high-speed packaging machine that was absolutely crucial to getting a major new product to market on time. As I was touring the line, the production operator said to me, "I was sweating bullets until this line got started." And I said, "You and me both."

I was so impressed by this man's level of commitment. He recognized how important the project was to the success of the company. I give a lot of credit to the people who lead that manufacturing operation. They have been able to create an environment where the people on the line really believe they can make a major contribution.

Zaleznik: That desire to contribute, that desire to be sent in, really is hardwired in us. It came before there was such a thing as a paycheck or a bonus payment. And for me that raises the issue of extrinsic rewards and intrinsic rewards. I think a paycheck buys you a baseline level of performance. But one thing that makes a good leader is the ability to offer people intrinsic rewards, the tremendous lift that comes from being aware of one's own talents and wanting to maximize them.

Talent is something that we don't talk about enough. As a psychoanalyst, I often encounter people who feel as if they're floating through life. They have no sense of desire. They cannot answer the question, what am I good at? Anybody who works with adolescents or has adolescent children knows that this is one of the toughest questions there is. What a leader can do is show people by example how to answer it. If a leader has a sense of his talent and respects it, and is driven to make the most of it, this creates a contagion effect.

For instance, some people are able to look at a product and immediately sense that it isn't going to meet the needs of the people who are going to use it. And then they're able to spot the anomalies, improve the design, and create a product that people will buy. This takes imagination, acute observation, and the ability to internalize observations and use them to come up with new ideas. This is a tremendously exciting enterprise. And leaders who can pass on that excitement to their followers are tapping into the contagious power of identification, which I mentioned earlier. If you have it, people will ask themselves, "What am I good at? How can I hone my talents and make them work for me and for other people?"

Tragge-Lakra: People setting out on the leadership path need to ask themselves something similar. The first piece of advice we give to people who come to GE's management training center in Crotonville, New York, is, "Get to know your own style." We try to help each person discover how he or she is most effective as a leader. Some people are comfortable with a forceful approach, where they come in and give a lot of strong direction right from the outset. Others are more comfortable with a more participatory approach. They'd rather get a lot of input and touch a lot of bases before they start setting a course.

Whatever their styles, we can show them the kinds of meetings and review processes that play to their advantages. But we also remind people that they can't always rely on their strengths. There are going to be times when they have to step out of their comfort zones.

Smith: Getting uncomfortable comes with the leadership territory. Leaders need to be flexible and adaptable, and sometimes that means doing things differently from what you're accustomed to. You don't change everything. The principles of leadership are pretty well established. So are the principles of followership, for that matter. They're really the mirror image of leadership. When someone joins an organization, they have five questions: What do you expect from me? What's in it for me? Where do I go if I have a problem? How am I doing? And is what I'm doing important? You always have to answer those five questions, but you have to adapt your leadership style to the situation at hand. Younger people look at the world differently from people of my generation, for example, and you have to modify your style to fit this different outlook. We didn't have things like telecommuting and job sharing when I was starting out in business, but it's something that's very important to many of our younger employees. Times change and people's needs change, and we have to be flexible enough to accommodate them, as long as we don't compromise our values and our standards.

Hesselbein: You can also use your organizational structure to develop leaders. Instead of a sort of pyramid with one little guy looking down while the other people look up, you have something that looks more like a series of concentric circles. The tasks of leadership are dispersed across the organization, which releases a phenomenal amount of energy. And that's the leader's job, after all: not to provide energy but to release it from others.

Tiger: You need to be careful, though, to put your developing leaders in situations where it's clear they're there to lead, not to contend for dominance. All the energy and ambition and productivity that make someone a good candidate for leadership development can be very destructive when he or she is pointed at the wrong target. Allow me to describe a lyrical piece of work done by one of the world's experts on chicken behavior, Glenn McBride, who's from Australia. Glenn was called in by egg producers there who were having trouble with their chickens. The egg producers had noticed that some chickens laid bigger eggs than others. They figured, logically enough, that it was stupid to have chickens that laid small eggs. Why not have only chickens that laid big eggs? So they acquired chickens that laid big eggs and put them in a chicken coop. And lo and behold, they started pecking each other to death. The producers called Dr. McBride, who pointed out that big eggs are produced by dominant chickens. Too many dominants had been put in one pen, and they were killing each other. There's a parallel, I think, to the rivalries and power struggles that erupt in the business world from time to time.

Gilmartin: There's an inevitable amount of rivalry that's going to occur when you have two people competing for one spot, and that's not all bad. But you can avoid really vicious, distracting power struggles by choosing the right leadership candidates in the first place. In selecting leaders for Merck, my goal is to have everyone in the organization agree that I picked exactly the right person for the job. And in making that selection, the will to dominate counts for a lot less than an ability and a willingness to solve problems. Leaders have to be comfortable with the idea of having a continuous stream of problems to solve. When I was less experienced, I would say, "After I get past this problem, everything out there will be happiness and peace." Then I realized that happiness and peace come from knowing that whatever problem is brought to me, I—or someone in the company—can solve it. But this is why some people don't want to assume leadership roles, because people only come to you when there is a problem. You have to enjoy the problems.

HBR: *Yes, but aren't some problems too serious and scary to enjoy? How do you handle those?*

Gilmartin: You're right—some problems aren't fun at all. But for the good of the organization, you can't let them throw you. I was in my office one day a few years ago, and someone came in with unexpected news that could have had a significant impact on the company. In the face of news like that, you have to be unflappable. You have to show that you understand completely the seriousness of the situation. But at the same time, a leader has to create an environment where people can get to work on solving the problem. It's very important to the organization that you face these situations with some sort of personal courage. If I had panicked, if I had said, "How could you have let this happen?" everyone would have frozen.

Tiger: There are some findings in primatology that have some bearing here. In chimp troops, the leader is at the center of the troop and is taking in information from all sides, from the male chimps at the edges of the troop, guarding and surveying, and from the females and their young. In fact, the attention structure of a primate group, not the distribution of resources, will tell you who is the leader. It's not who gets the most bananas—it's who gets looked at. Every 30 seconds or so, the chimps are orienting to the leader. If the leader's central nervous system isn't really calm, the other chimps get agitated and can't do their jobs. [For an extended discussion of the wide-ranging effects of the leader's mood, see Chapter 2, "Primal Leadership: The Hidden Driver of Great Performance."]

How the leader maintains his calm is what's really interesting. Mike McGuire, who is at the UCLA Neuropsychiatric Institute, has done some work with monkeys and serotonin, the compound that produces a sense of calm and well-being and confidence. It turns out that leader primates have decisively higher levels of serotonin. McGuire's first notion was that leaders are born with elevated serotonin levels. But that turned out not to be the case. He found that when he removed the leaders from their troops, their serotonin levels crashed to well below the norm. Then, once a new leader emerged, its serotonin level started climbing until it was twice that of the other primates. An elevated level appears to be an adaptation to the stresses and uncertainties of the leadership role. And it's an adaptation that benefits the troop as well as the leader. The distinguishing characteristic of leaders is the quality of their central nervous system in a crisis. And serotonin enables the central nervous system to handle stress and ambiguity.

Gilmartin: Is that why we like the job so much?

Smith: What you call being unflappable, Ray, sounds more like courage to me. Leaders have to be capable of dealing with danger—maybe not actual physical danger but problems and issues that demand a fair bit of courage. I mean, I can be totally unflappable and be absolutely stupid. But seeing a threat coming down and staying calm, now, that's a different matter. Your organization needs to see you maintain your calm, but people also need to see that your calm is accompanied by a lot of activity. You have to be decisive, set clear directions, and keep moving. You have to show you're not immobilized by crisis.

The best leadership advice I ever got came from a sergeant when I was a young Marine lieutenant just arrived in Vietnam. He said, "If you want to know how to lead your troops, there are just three things you have to remember: Shoot. Move. Communicate." In a business context, I think that means that you have to be decisive. You have to pick a target and go for it. You can't stand still and present an easy target for your enemies. And communicate means, well, communicate. The best way to look after your people is to keep them informed, even if you have to deliver bad news. If you're looking for the essentials of leadership, there they are.

The Participants

Frances Hesselbein. Former CEO of the Girl Scouts and chairman of the Peter F. Drucker Foundation

Lionel Tiger. The Charles Darwin Professor of Anthropology at Rutgers University

Raymond Gilmartin. Chairman and CEO of Merck & Company

Frederick Smith. Chairman and CEO of FedEx

Cynthia Tragge-Lakra. Manager of executive development at General Electric

Abraham Zaleznik. The Konosuke Matsushita Professor of Leadership, Emeritus, at Harvard Business School

Originally published in December 2001
Reprint R0111D

What Titans Can Teach Us

RICHARD S. TEDLOW

Executive Summary

THE LEGENDARY TITANS of American business could be scheming and ruthless. We surely wouldn't want to emulate them in every particular. But a business leader doesn't have to strive for titanhood to benefit from the lessons such giants have to teach. And perhaps by studying them, we can learn to spot titans in the making, a valuable skill for leaders scanning the landscape for potential partners or dangerous competitors.

Focusing on the experiences of seven great innovators—steel magnate Andrew Carnegie, Kodak's George Eastman, automaker Henry Ford, Intel's Robert Noyce, Revlon's Charles Revson, Wal-Mart's Sam Walton, and IBM's Thomas J. Watson—the author argues that many of their traits are replicable by mere mortals. A handful of simple principles were woven into their lives: Have the courage to bet on your vision of market potential. Shape your vision of the market into a mission for the company and consistent messages for customers, employees, and investors. Deliver more than you promise. Be dedicated to your company, even to a fault. And don't look back.

Enlivening his narrative with such details as Walton's hula dance on Wall Street and Eastman's succinct suicide note—"My work is done—why wait?"—the author shows that the titans thought about their companies every waking moment and expected the same of their employees. They were willing to pay whatever price was needed to create something new in the business world.

Whether they led through inspiration or intimidation, a clear mission and consistent messages were keys to making their dreams reality. So were a limitless sense of what they had to offer and an unflinching commitment to the fulfillment of their destinies. Their certainty in the face of uncertainty, skepticism, and even ridicule was a beacon for attracting and motivating followers.

FIRST THINGS FIRST: I'm not going to make the case in this article that the legendary titans of American business offer a template of leadership lessons for all of us to follow. Many were individuals we wouldn't want to emulate, at least in every particular. They could be scheming and, more than occasionally, ruthless. Indeed, in many instances they were as titanic in the problems they created—especially the interpersonal problems—as in the empires they built.

Furthermore, most of us couldn't emulate these legends even if we tried. They were wildly opportunistic, ambitious beyond measure, and often just plain brilliant. While these attributes are useful and even admirable for

businesspeople, the genuine giants of enterprise had
them to a unique degree—which partly explains why
they were titans and most other people are not.

That said, a business leader doesn't have to strive for
titanhood to benefit from the lessons a titan has to teach.
We can pick and choose the characteristics that will help
make our companies more successful. Perhaps just as
important, we can learn to spot titans in the making, a
valuable skill for leaders scanning the landscape for
potential business partners or successors—or on the
lookout for dangerous competitors.

What do I mean by "titan?" For me, the term encom-
passes those executives—there have been perhaps 30 or
40 in the history of American business—who created or
transformed industries and in the process changed the
world. All of them grew rich as they did so. Most of them
became household names. Is someone like Jack Welch a
member of this elite club? The answer: We just don't
know yet. You can only identify a titan with historical
perspective—which is what makes the subject so fasci-
nating for me, a business historian.

For the past three decades, I have studied the giants of
American enterprise. Using my database of detailed
biographical and com-
pany information on 250
outstanding business
executives, I have identified the individuals
whom I call titans and
then looked for common
denominators among

*A defining characteristic
of the titans was their ability
to tell the difference
between the seemingly
impossible and the
genuinely impossible.*

the select few. This article draws on the experiences of
seven of the titans: steel magnate Andrew Carnegie;
George Eastman, the father of mass-market photography;

automaker Henry Ford; IBM's Thomas J. Watson; Charles Revson, founder of cosmetics maker Revlon; Wal-Mart's Sam Walton; and Robert Noyce, the cofounder of Intel.

These seven were very different people. Eastman and Noyce led primarily through inspiration; Carnegie and Watson led mainly by intimidation. Walton, the optimist, could light up a room; Revson, the pessimist, could light up a room by leaving it. Noyce helped ensure a successful future for Intel by working in close partnership with two successors, Gordon Moore and Andy Grove, whose talents complemented his and suited the company in its next stages of growth. Ford, by contrast, became vindictive as he aged and nearly destroyed his company. (Different though they were, we must note that they were all not only male but also Caucasian. There are women and minorities in business today whom future generations will regard as titans, but their impact on the business scene is too recent to permit the historical perspective we need to make that judgment.)

Though titans are a varied lot, we can still tease some common traits out of their disparate personalities and lives. Some of these reflect their particular genius. For example, a defining characteristic of these men was their ability to tell the difference between the seemingly impossible and the genuinely impossible. Other traits are similarly relevant to their business success but are more replicable by mere mortals. In studying their careers, we can see a handful of principles that were woven into their lives:

- Have the courage to bet on your vision of market potential.

- Shape your vision of the market into a mission for the company and consistent messages for customers, employees, and investors.

- Deliver more than you promise.

- Be dedicated, even to a fault, to your company.

- Don't look back.

The following stories—yes, stories; I'm a historian, not a management consultant—illustrate ways in which the titans lived these five principles. I would not advise anyone to try to mimic a particular titan. But they did drive their companies to success with stunning power. What they did worked, and there is plenty they can teach us.

A Camera for Everyone

George Eastman seems an unlikely creator of mass-market photography, an innovation that enabled ordinary people to create visual records of their lives without the expense of hiring professional photographers or portrait painters. His first job was as an office boy in an insurance firm—the death of his debt-ridden father and the straitened financial circumstances of his family had forced him to go to work in 1868 at the age of 13. He was paid $3 a week, and his responsibilities included cleaning out the cuspidors.

Not long thereafter, Eastman took a job as a clerk at the Rochester (New York) Savings Bank, where he quickly moved up to second assistant bookkeeper. In 1877, after spending almost a decade in the working world, he bought a camera. Four years later, he left the bank to devote himself fully to starting a photography business. Eventually, his business would transform the complicated contraptions used by professional photographers into light little boxes anyone could afford.

Even after he threw himself exclusively into photography, it took time for Eastman to comprehend that there was a mass market for picture taking. When he started in the business, cameras were expensive, costing roughly $50. They required considerable expertise to operate. Few people in the early 1880s even thought about taking photographs. But what if photography could be made both cheap and easy? No one knew. No one even knew this was a question worth asking.

In the late 1880s, though, Eastman began to believe that he "could reach the general public and create a new class of patrons"—that is, democratize photography while creating a lucrative new market. "Success," he wrote in 1890, "means millions." In 1894, he said that "the manifest destiny of the Eastman Kodak Company is to be the largest manufacturer of photographic materials in the world or else go to pot." In 1900, Eastman brought out the Kodak Brownie, which sold for $1. One of the great product introductions in American business history, the Brownie allowed Eastman to realize his vision: photography for everyone.

How did Eastman know there was a mass market for photography when few people had ever seen a camera? Similarly, how did Carnegie know that steel, once sold by the pound, would in the new industrialized world be sold by the ton? How did Ford know to stick with low-priced cars in the early years of the industry when rival automakers in America and Europe kept moving upmarket? How did Watson know that the future lay in the small branch of his company that made tabulating machines? How did Revson know in 1932, during the depths of the Depression, that there was a profitable market for high-fashion nail polish? How did Walton know that small towns could support big stores? How did Noyce know that the integrated circuit, of which he was the coinventor, would change the world?

They just knew. They sensed they were on to something. It's as simple, and as complex, as that—not very encouraging for those trying to emulate their success. An intuitive sense of market potential is not the sort of thing you can study hard to learn.

But if the titans possessed that jagged streak of lightning called genius, they also had something else: Each had the courage to bet on his vision. Achieving a breakthrough insight is one thing. Acting on it is quite another. These monumental figures were more than men of potential, they were kinetic. They refused to be scared off by precedent.

Eastman's actions reflected his belief that his company's "manifest destiny" was to succeed on a grand scale. Walton, who built giant Wal-Mart stores across the land and around the world, wasn't deterred by the fact that no one saw a huge retailing opportunity in rural areas and small towns. Ford didn't care that the United States had few passable roads for his new automobile. As Noyce once said, "Don't be encumbered by history. Go out and do something wonderful."

Hula on Wall Street

The date was March 15, 1984. The place was Wall Street, the financial capital of the world. The man was Samuel Moore Walton, at the time the nation's second-richest citizen. The event was a hula performance.

Walton had made a bet with his chief operating officer, David Glass, that Wal-Mart could not achieve a pretax profit of 8% on sales. In 1983, the company met that target, and Glass insisted that Walton keep his promise to do the hula on Wall Street. And this bet was not going to be paid off on the sly in the dark of night. Glass saw to it that there was a grass skirt for Walton to put on over his suit, musicians and young professional hula dancers to accompany him, and, of course, full media attention.

By this time, Walton and Wal-Mart were well known and respected in the investment community and throughout a large part of the nation. But here was the company's CEO flying in from Arkansas and engaging in what Walton himself later characterized as a "pretty primitive publicity stunt." Although such stunts—at stores, at headquarters, for customers, for suppliers, for employees, for the media—were a staple at Wal-Mart, Walton had to confess that this particular display genuinely embarrassed him.

Why, then, did he do it? True, he had made a bet and had lost. But no one could have forced Sam Walton to pay up. He could have said that it wasn't appropriate for the CEO of one of the nation's fastest-growing companies to make a fool of himself in the middle of the financial district. He could have cited his age, 65, and his recent bout with leukemia—not to mention the 28-degree temperature on the day of the dance. Or he could have simply let Glass know that if he liked working for the leading retailer in Bentonville, Arkansas, he'd better let the bet die a quiet death. But despite his wealth and power, Walton kept his promise—and he did it to make a point.

Or rather several points. Sam (one naturally falls into referring to this multibillionaire by his first name) originally saw a market opportunity in offering customers outside big cities quality goods at low prices. This vision became the company's mission, which was articulated in a memorable message: "Always the low price—*always*." Clearly, a key to maintaining low prices is keeping costs down. So instead of taking out an ad in the *Wall Street*

Journal, Walton publicized Wal-Mart's achievement with a publicity device that cost almost nothing. A penny saved on advertising was a penny that could be passed along to the customer. In fact, the main cost associated with the event was to Walton's dignity—which he would never have placed above the good of the company.

But Walton had more than customers in mind when he did his hula. For decades, he had been preaching to employees that rank does not have its privileges. In his mind, the thousands of salespeople on the floor were as important as top executives, because Wal-Mart's primary contact with its customers was through these low-wage employees. His dance signaled that he was a down-to-earth guy who didn't have an inflated view of himself.

By showing up in a hula skirt on Wall Street, Sam Walton showed he was willing to put the company's interests above his own—just as he wanted his employees to do.

Walton also praised outlandish behavior among employees because it stimulated creativity and helped make Wal-Mart "a fun proposition." He endlessly insisted that you could learn from anybody, and having fun was one way that the thousands of anybodies at Wal-Mart did their teaching. Walton had a special genius for transforming anybodies into somebodies. When the silly season rolled around, Walton didn't merely cheer from the sidelines, he was a player-coach.

Finally, Walton showed employees that he was willing to put the company's interests above his own—just as he wanted them to do. He knew that the speed of the boss is the speed of the gang, and his sense of fairness would not permit him to demand that others sacrifice for the company if he were unwilling to do so.

The hula wasn't staged on Wall Street by chance. There was also a message for investors and analysts: I may not look like the most sophisticated executive in the world, but I'm a winner. Actions speak louder than words, and losers don't pull stunts like this. Margaret Gilliam, at the time an analyst for First Boston and one of the first to realize that Wal-Mart was a company with a future, did not have to travel far to photograph Sam in his grass skirt.

By walking his talk, Walton, in a single act, sent multiple messages to multiple constituencies. Although other titans may have used more conventional means, they all had a similar missionary zeal, which they communicated through clear and consistent messages.

George Eastman's ambition to bring photography to the people was reflected in the advertising slogan for the Brownie: "You push the button. We do the rest." Pithy to the point of poetry, it communicated to customers that photography was no longer a mysterious black art presided over by secretive professionals telling you to keep perfectly still while they mixed miraculous concoctions of chemicals to make your image appear on a glass plate.

Tom Watson's mission for IBM employees was reduced to a single word: Think. Or, more accurately, THINK. The word reflected the intellectual foundation of the technology-driven company.

Tom Watson's mission for IBM employees was reduced to a single word: think. Or, more accurately, THINK. The word reflected the technology-driven company's intellectual foundation. (It also said something about Watson's leadership style. When he plastered THINK signs all over the company, he wasn't saying, "Think for yourself." There was no mistaking he meant, "Think like me.")

A Giant Pay Raise

On January 5, 1914, Henry Ford stood by quietly in his office as an associate read a news release to reporters from three Detroit newspapers:

"The Ford Motor Co., the greatest and most successful automobile manufacturing company in the world, will, on Jan. 12, inaugurate the greatest revolution in the matter of rewards for its workers ever known to the industrial world. At one stroke it will reduce the hours of labor from nine to eight, and add to every man's pay a share of the profits of the house. The smallest amount to be received by a man 22 years old and upwards will be $5 per day."

The language of the press release was self-congratulatory, but deservedly so. Three months earlier, Ford workers had received a 13% wage increase to $2.34 a day. Now, without violence, without pressure from a union, the company was more than doubling an already competitive wage.

Ford saw the press release as merely a good local story, so he distributed it only to the local press. But it became the biggest news story to originate in Detroit up to that time, and it made Henry Ford famous around the world.

There were, it should be said, business reasons for the big jump in workers' salaries. Because of growing mechanization, work in the plant was becoming increasingly stultifying; the turnover rate at Ford was a staggering 370% in 1913. A more stable and better-paid workforce could—and ultimately did—result in production efficiencies. But these were not the only reasons for the pay hike. Henry Ford simply felt it was the thing to do. As one newspaper described him at the time, he "has declined to forget that the distance between overalls and broadcloth is very short." With the pay raise, he was delivering far more than he had promised—indeed, more than any of his employees might have reasonably expected.

The titans delivered more than they promised to investors, as well. The sister of one of Ford's first partners put $100 into his company. Less than two decades later, Rosetta Couzens Hauss, a schoolteacher in Chatham, Ontario, received $262,036.67 for that $100. And true titans could generate big rewards for investors even when their companies encountered bumps along the road. One Intel manager recalls the faith that the investment community placed in Noyce: "Bob could stand up in front of a roomful of securities analysts and tell them we were facing a number of major problems in our business—and the stock would go up five points."

More subtly, the breakthrough products or services that the titans created also delivered more than customers ever expected. During the Depression, Revson introduced the Revlon brand of coordinated nail polish and lipstick, which gave women "matching lips and fingertips." Helena Rubinstein derided the brightly colored nail polish as trashy. But by turning nail enamel from a commodity into a fashion item, he gave women of modest means an unexpected way to feel special. As Revson said, "in the factory, we make cosmetics; in the store, we sell hope."

Split Personality

Andrew Carnegie is one of the most seductive of the business titans. He embodied the American dream, rising from rags not to riches—but to richest. In 1848, Carnegie was forced to emigrate from Scotland, where his father, a hand-loom weaver, had been put out of work by the technology of steam power. Carnegie would go on to master, rather than be mastered by, technology.

At 13, he got a job at $1.20 a week in a steam-driven textile mill in Pittsburgh. He left to work in a telegraph office and taught himself Morse code. His next move was to the Pennsylvania Railroad, the spine of American enterprise in the mid-nineteenth century. With the help of Tom Scott, a mentor who became a surrogate father, Carnegie quickly rose to become superintendent of the railroad's western division. By the time of the Civil War, Carnegie had mastered the two forces that were changing the world: the telegraph and the railroad.

After making a small fortune as an investor during the 1860s, Carnegie was hit with a searing insight. Technological breakthroughs, most notably the Bessemer process, opened up the possibility of producing steel in undreamed-of quantities. Knowing railroads and their desperate need for strong, all-weather rails, Carnegie was convinced that steel would change the material basis of civilization in the last quarter of the nineteenth century. His conviction proved justified.

Carnegie was charming and witty with a puckish sense of humor. Unlike contemporary "robber barons" such as J.P. Morgan or John D. Rockefeller, he wanted to be liked and knew how to make himself likable. However, he had neither compunction nor hesitation about breaking the eggs that went into his omelette.

Take his early mentor, Tom Scott, the man who lifted Carnegie out of the obscurity of a telegraph office and into the upper reaches of the Pennsylvania Railroad, who taught the unschooled immigrant how to invest and financed his first investment. In 1873, when Scott came to him for financial help to stave off bankruptcy, the wealthy Carnegie summarily turned him down. He could be similarly strict with his partners—who were partners in name only. Carnegie owned the majority of his company and doled out dividends parsimoniously. His partners worked long days while he took extended vacations.

Perhaps most telling, Carnegie was ruthless with the workers in his gigantic mills. He fancied himself a great friend of labor. "My experience," he wrote in 1886, "has been that trades-unions, upon the whole, are beneficial both to labor and to capital." He also declared that there "is an unwritten law among the best workmen: 'Thou shalt not take thy neighbor's job.'" Not many employers were saying that sort of thing in 1886, and Carnegie was lionized among workers in many industries.

Six years later, Carnegie, conveniently on vacation in Britain, allowed his partner Henry Clay Frick to break the union at the company's Homestead Plant. Pinkerton detectives were hired. Scab labor was brought in. Lives were lost. The Amalgamated Association of Iron and Steel Workers met with complete defeat. As one of Carnegie's executives put it, "The Amalgamated placed a tax on improvements, therefore the Amalgamated had to go."

Like most of America's business titans, Carnegie paid a high personal price for his complete dedication to his company's success and to his own ambition. The price for him was the sharp split between what he wanted to be—or at least saw himself as—and what tremendous success in business demanded that he be. Carnegie sought the affection of his

The titans led their companies to greatness by thinking about them every waking moment. George Eastman committed suicide and left a note that read: "To my friends: My work is done—why wait?"

friends, partners, and workers. Yet, in the end, he alienated many because his loyalty was to his company first, last, and above all.

Carnegie was not alone among the titans in his single-minded dedication to his ambition. Most of them had wives, clubs, hobbies, and philanthropic endeavors. But they led their companies to greatness by thinking about them every waking moment and by expecting the same from their employees. They were willing to pay the price needed to create something new in the business world.

Tom Watson retired from IBM in May 1956—and died in June 1956, having refused potentially lifesaving surgery for an intestinal problem. George Eastman committed suicide and left a note that read: "To my friends: My work is done—why wait?" Eastman's note may have been a bit misleading. At 77, he hadn't worked regularly for years. He had traveled extensively to foreign countries in his retirement. His health was failing. But the sentiments certainly captured the fact that, as with Watson, his company had been the center of his life.

It is perhaps noteworthy that Eastman, unlike some other titans, didn't let an all-encompassing focus on the success of his business undermine his personal values and friendships. As Eastman's first financial backer and partner observed, "You are a queer cuss, Geo, and I know you never want any sympathy or comfort from your friends. But I want you to know that I, for one, appreciate the mountains of care and responsibility that you are constantly called to overcome. And if I never express it in words, it may be a source of comfort to you to know that I am always with you heart and hand."

Starting Over at 40

John Patterson, the founder of National Cash Register Company and Tom Watson's first boss, dealt with people in three stages. First, he shattered a man's spirit and obliterated his previous identity and self-conception. Then he built him up, buttressed his self-esteem, and paid him lavishly. Then he fired him.

That's a fair description of Watson's career path at NCR. He joined the company as a salesman in Buffalo, New York, in 1895 when he was 21. He devoted himself to NCR and its mercurial leader, doing whatever it took to get ahead, for almost two decades. In 1913, he found his head on the chopping block.

It wasn't, to put it mildly, an easy period in Watson's life. He was 40 years old and newly married with an infant son. He also had serious legal problems, having been convicted, along with other NCR executives, of criminal violations of the Sherman Act for his unquestioning adherence to some of Patterson's less attractive business practices. Although the conviction was later overturned on appeal, Watson at the time faced a year in jail and a $5,000 fine.

Watson took a job with an unknown company called Computing-Tabulating-Recording, a motley and directionless conglomerate that made scales (computing), adding and sorting machines (tabulating), and time clocks (recording). Soon he was running the company, rechristened International Business Machines. His focus on the relatively small tabulating division put IBM on the road to becoming the preeminent name in what came to be known as computers. Significantly, Watson didn't carry a grudge against Patterson, who taught him many of the sales techniques that later contributed to IBM's success. As Thomas J. Watson, Jr., Watson's son and successor as CEO at IBM, once remarked: "Oddly, Dad never complained [of Patterson's firing him] and revered Mr. Patterson until the day he died."

Titans don't look back. When they suffer a failure, they get over it. Most know the valleys as well as the peaks—but they never perceive a chasm, no matter how daunting, to be the Valley of Death. They don't ruminate. They are incapable of being discouraged.

And whatever problems they have faced in the past, they're not afraid of the future, because they plan to play a big role in creating it. While not necessarily arrogant, they do have staggering confidence in themselves. For example, when William Shockley, the famed coinventor of the transistor, asked the unknown Bob Noyce to interview for a job at his new semiconductor company, Noyce left his job at Philco in Philadelphia and bought a house in Palo Alto, California—*before* the interview. This self-confidence is contagious and serves the titan superbly well when things start going badly, as they did for every one of these men at one time or another.

For example, Intel's first two products, introduced in 1969, were technically advanced but commercially unsuccessful. Rumors began to circulate that if Intel didn't have a success soon, it would be in trouble. Undaunted, Noyce pressed on, and Intel brought out the first in a long string of blockbuster products. Eastman was passed over for first assistant bookkeeper at the Rochester Savings Bank because of nepotism. Eastman, who had an acute sense of fairness, was outraged. Walton lost his first store—a thriving five-and-dime in Newport, Arkansas—to the landlord's son because he failed to notice that his lease didn't include a renewal clause. Ford founded two companies that failed before he created the Ford Motor Company. Revson was living hand-to-mouth, thanks to a string of dead-end jobs, when he founded Revlon in 1932.

One clear lesson that everyone can take from the titans is that they didn't blame others—or the universe—for their problems. They may have been downcast or temporarily angry with themselves. But they didn't whine that life was unfair. They believed the world was essentially a just place that would reward their effort and, ultimately, yield to their genius. Any setback was a temporary misunderstanding by the cosmos.

There is no formula for business greatness. There are, however, themes that recur in the conduct of business titans. Whether they led through inspiration or intimidation, a clear mission and consistent messages were keys to making their dreams a reality. So were a limitless sense of what they had to offer and an unflinching commitment to the fulfillment of their destinies.

Their certainty in the face of an uncertain, sometimes derisive, world can be a beacon for attracting and motivating followers. Their message is not inclusive, however. The individuals I have studied didn't create organizations designed for everyone. If you wanted to work for one of them, you had to buy into the mission and spread the message. Otherwise, you belonged elsewhere.

As we have seen, there may be good reasons not to try to become a titan yourself. But whatever your aim, it's good to be able to recognize a titan. We can also take inspiration and ideas from these giants of enterprise and their common achievement: business success through the writing (and enforcing) of their own rules.

Originally published in December 2001
Reprint R0111E

The Hard Work of Being a Soft Manager

WILLIAM H. PEACE

Executive Summary

SOFT MANAGEMENT DOES NOT mean weak management. It means candor, openness, and vulnerability, but it also means hard choices and responsible follow-up. It means taking the heat for difficult decisions and giving unhappy subordinates a chance to unburden themselves at your expense.

In the early 1980's, when William Peace had to lay off 15 people at Westinghouse's threatened Synthetic Fuels Division, he insisted on meeting them in person, explaining management's reasons for the layoff, and giving each of them a chance to object, criticize, and vent their anger. Peace's action reassured the remaining employees that the division did not face immediate closure, and it so eased the emotional blow for those laid off that when the division got the chance to rehire some of them a few months later, every single one came back, including those who had found other jobs. By deliberately making himself vulnerable, Peace increased his credibility with all his employees.

In analyzing what had happened, Peace recalls the model for his actions. Years earlier, the general manager of another Westinghouse division troubled by low productivity and low profits made a series of informational presentations to workers so hostile they met his patient but persistent explanations of company problems with catcalls, insults, and abuse. Yet the upshot of the meetings was greater credibility for the general manager, a big improvement in labor-management relations, and increased productivity and profits.

In both cases, deliberate vulnerability and willingness to take the heat for unpopular positions brought unexpected benefits. Soft management is no job for the fainthearted, but it makes managers more human, more credible, and more open to change.

I AM A SOFT MANAGER. Unlike the classic leaders of business legend with their towering self-confidence, their unflinching tenacity, their hard, lonely lives at the top, I try to be vulnerable to criticism, I do my best to be tentative, and I cherish my own fair share of human frailty. But like them, I too have worked hard to master my management style, and, on the whole, I think it compares favorably with theirs.

In my vocabulary, soft management does not mean weak management. A tentative approach to a critical decision in an unfamiliar environment is not a sign of indecision but of common sense. Criticism from your subordinates is not necessarily a sign of disrespect; they may be offering the wisdom and experience of a different perspective.

Conversely, tough management does not necessarily mean effective management. Self-confidence can be a cover for arrogance or fear, resolute can be a code word for autocratic, and hard-nosed can mean thick-skinned.

I believe that openness is a productive management technique and that intentional vulnerability is an effective management style. The "soft" management I believe in and do my best to practice is a matter of making hard choices and of accepting personal responsibility for decisions. I have a couple of stories that illustrate what I mean.

In the early 1980s, I was general manager of the Synthetic Fuels Division of Westinghouse. Unfortunately, the decline in oil prices that followed the second oil shock in 1979 had led Westinghouse top management to decide to get out of the synthetic fuels business, so my staff and I had to find a buyer and consummate a sale within a few months or face the prospect of seeing our division dismantled and liquidated.

Self-confidence can be a cover for arrogance. Hard-nosed can mean thick-skinned.

In an effort to make ourselves attractive, we had already trimmed the work force from 240 to about 130, most of them engaged in the design, testing, and marketing of a coal gasification process that we were confident would one day produce electric power from coal efficiently, cleanly, and economically. While we believed in the technology, we realized that, in the midst of a recession, there weren't many buyers for energy businesses that could offer only future profits.

For the employees in the division, closure would mean more than unemployment. It would mean shattering the dream of building a great new business, a dream many of us had been working toward for more than five years. Unfortunately, even with the reduced work force we had a dilemma. The continuing financial drain we represented tended to shorten the corporation's patience, but if we cut employment too much, we would have nothing left to sell. Moreover, as winter approached, my staff and I became concerned that Westinghouse was about to set an absolute deadline for selling the division.

My senior managers and I approached this dilemma as gingerly as we could, with much discussion and no foregone conclusions. We decided that a further reduction in force of 15 people was both necessary to sustain the corporation's goodwill and tolerable, perhaps even desirable, from the point of view of selling the business. We then examined various alternatives for selecting the people to lay off. We agreed that our criteria would not include performance as such. Instead, we decided to choose jobs with the lowest probable value in the eyes of a potential buyer, provided only that they were not essential to the task of selling the business. For example, we decided we could get along with two technicians in the chemistry lab instead of three.

After about an hour of give-and-take, some of it heated, we agreed to a list of 15 names, and as the meeting drew to a close, one department head said to the others, "Well, let's go tell them." It had been our practice in past layoffs to choose an hour when all managers with people on the reduction list would call them in and give them the bad news.

"No," I said, "I'm going to tell them myself."

"But that's not necessary," someone said.

"I think it is necessary," I said.

I was concerned that a further reduction in force might lead the remaining employees to conclude that management had given up on selling the business and that it was only a matter of time before we laid off everyone else as well and closed the business down. If they were to draw that conclusion, many of our most valuable people would leave. During months of uncertainty about the future of the division, our best engineering and marketing people had located opportunities with other companies, and they were now sitting on those offers waiting to see what would happen to Synthetic Fuels. They needed to hear the real reasons for the layoffs from me—personally.

I asked my senior managers to send all employees on the reduction-in-force list to a conference room early the following morning. I wanted to explain as truthfully as I could what it was we were doing and why.

Walking into the conference room the next morning was like walking into a funeral home. The 15 employees sat around the table in mourning. Most of the women were crying. Most of the men, stunned and dejected, were staring at the tabletop. Their managers sat in chairs against the wall, clearly wishing they were somewhere else. I had not expected my staff to announce the purpose of the meeting, but, obviously, people knew.

I summoned my courage and took the chair at the head of the table. I told the employees we were going to lay them off and that all of us, I in particular, felt very bad about it. I went through our reasoning on the reduction in force, putting particular emphasis on our belief that this RIF would improve our chances of selling the division—as opposed to closing it. I told them we were, in effect, sacrificing a few for the benefit of many. I explained the criteria we had used and observed that while we felt our thinking was sound and believed we had matched people to the criteria in good faith, we understood that they might well disagree. I said we were doing the best we could—imperfect as that might be—to save the business. I asked them not to blame their managers. I ordered them not to blame themselves—our decision was in no way a value judgment on them as individuals, I said. If they wanted someone to blame, I urged them to blame me.

These remarks took about 15 minutes, and then I asked for questions. The initial responses were all attempts to discredit the selection process. "But why *aren't* you taking performance into account?" one woman asked. "My supervisor has told me my performance is excellent. What's the point of doing a good job if you only get laid off?"

"I've been here for 11 years," said a male technician. "Why shouldn't I get more consideration than someone who was hired only a couple of years ago?"

I responded by repeating that under the circumstances, we believed only two criteria were relevant: first, that the position be nonessential to the selling process and, second, that it be one that prospective buyers would see as having relatively little value to them in the short term.

The questions kept coming, and for a time the tearful, funereal mood persisted, but eventually other questions began to surface. Did we really think the division could be sold? Did we think there really was a future for synthetic fuels? Why couldn't Westinghouse wait a little longer? The question period went on for a good 45 minutes and was without doubt one of the most painful I've ever attended. And yet, as it ended, I felt a certain new closeness to those 15 people. I shook hands with each of them and wished them good luck. I thought I sensed that most of them understood and even respected what we were trying to do, however much they might object to our final choice of sacrificial lambs.

For weeks the meeting stayed fresh in my mind. We'd hear, for example, that now Nancy's husband had been laid off from *his* job, and I would remember Nancy sitting at the conference table with tears streaming down her face, and the memory would be so bleak

When we got a chance to rehire people we'd laid off, every single one agreed to come back.

that I'd think, "Why did I insist on meeting with all of them myself? Why didn't I just let their bosses break the news?"

At the same time, however, I was beginning to notice a change I hadn't expected: the remaining employees seemed to have a renewed determination to hold the business together. For example, tests on the pilot plant continued with a new optimism; whenever I was in the test structure, the technicians seemed cheerful, positive, and entirely focused on the task at hand. And at a meeting to discuss the status of another project we wanted to hold onto, not only was the lead engineer still with us—pockets undoubtedly filled with attractive offers from oil companies—but he was explaining his ideas for reducing the project's capital costs.

A couple of months later, we did finally sell the business, and what happened next was even more gratifying. The new owner gave us funds for some additional work, and we suddenly had the chance to rehire about half of the 15 people we'd laid off. *Without exception*, they accepted our offers to return. One or two even gave up other jobs they'd found in the meantime. One secretary gave up a good position with a very stable and reputable local company to rejoin her friends at our still somewhat risky operation with all its grand dreams.

It gradually became apparent to me that my very painful meeting with those 15 employees had been a kind of turning point for Synthetic Fuels. Clearly, this was due in part to the two messages I sent in that meeting on behalf of senior management—first, that we would do everything in our power to keep the business alive and salable and, second, that we saw layoffs as an extremely regrettable last resort. But as time goes by, I am more and more convinced that the "success" of that meeting was also due in part to the fact that it made me vulnerable to the criticism, disapproval, and anger of the people we were laying off. If that sounds cryptic, let me explain by telling another story, a story I remembered only later when I began to analyze what had happened at Synthetic Fuels.

In the early 1970s, I worked for the vice president of the Westinghouse Steam Turbine Division, which was located just south of the Philadelphia airport in a sprawling complex of factories that had employed more than 10,000 people during World War II and was still a union stronghold. My boss, Gene Cattabiani, then in his forties, had a reputation as a good engineer and a "people person." In fact, his success in previous assignments had had much to do with his ability to get along with the people above and below him.

One of the most difficult issues facing Gene at Steam Turbine was an extremely hostile labor-relations environment. In the 1950s, the Union of Electrical Workers represented the entire hourly work force. It was a tough, unfriendly union, so much so that the McCarthy hearings had labeled it communist.

I had seen two faces of this union. On the one hand, its leaders were as stubborn as mules at the negotiating table, and its strikes were daunting. Several men once threatened to throw a small boulder through my windshield when I tried to cross a picket line to get to work. In 1956, the violent, confrontational mood of one nine-month strike led to a shooting death outside the plant.

On the other hand, I had also seen thoughtfulness and warmth. One year when I was chairman of the United Way campaign, we asked the union leaders to serve with me on the organizing committee. It was a very successful campaign, partly because they worked so hard to get the hourly work force to contribute, though few had ever given in the past.

By and large, however, attitudes were polarized. Most managers viewed shop floor workers as lazy and greedy, a distinct business liability. On their side, most union members viewed management as incompetent, overpaid, and more or less unnecessary.

When Gene took over, the Steam Turbine Division was not particularly profitable. There was a compelling need to cut costs and improve productivity, and it was clear that much of the opportunity for improvement was on the shop floor. Yet the historic animosities between labor and management made it seem unlikely that any fruitful negotiation could take place.

Gene decided it was up to him to break this impasse and begin to change attitudes on both sides by treating union leaders and the work force with respect, honesty, and openness. To me this made a great deal of sense. If managers began treating union members as human beings, with dignity and worth, they might just respond by treating us the same way.

But it was not just a matter of style. The business was in trouble, and unless the union understood the extent of the problem, it would have little incentive to cooperate. Historically, union leaders had assumed that the business was very profitable. They believed their people deserved a thick slice of what was in their view a large pie. By the time Gene arrived, however, the pie had become pretty skimpy and was threatening to vanish altogether. Gene decided it was essential to inform the union of the real state of the business.

In the past when there was any informing to be done, the labor-relations vice president would call a meeting with the union leadership and *tell* them what he wanted them to know. Not surprisingly, since they saw everything management said as entirely self-serving, union leaders had always viewed these meetings with disdain. This time, however, Gene decided he would do it differently. He would give a presentation on the state of the business to the entire hourly work force, a thing that had never been done in the long history of the division.

Many of us wondered if this was really necessary. We knew the rank and file saw the vice president and general manager—Gene—as the ultimate enemy. Wouldn't it be easier, we wondered, and maybe more effective, to have someone else make the presentation? Maybe they would listen to the financial manager. But Gene clung—stubbornly, I thought—to his decision.

To reach the entire work force, Gene would have to repeat the presentation several times to groups of hundreds of workers. The format was a slide presentation, simple but complete and clear, followed by questions from the floor.

The initial presentation was a nightmare. Gene wanted the work force to see that the business was in trouble, real trouble, and that their jobs depended on a different kind of relationship with management. But the workers assumed that management was up to its usual self-serving tricks, and there on stage, for the first time, they had the enemy in person. They heckled him mercilessly all through the slide show. Then, during the question-and-answer period, they shouted abuse and threats. As far as I could tell, they weren't hearing Gene's message—or even listening. I felt sure he had made a mistake in deciding to give the presentation himself.

But Gene persisted. With obvious dread but with grim determination, he made the full series of presentations. While I could see no evidence that people even understood his state-of-the-business message, much less believed it, I did begin to see an important change. When Gene went out on the factory floor for a look around (which his predecessors never did unless they were giving customers a tour), people began to offer a nod of recognition—a radical change from the way they used to spit on the floor as he walked by.

Gene had ceased to be an ordinary useless manager and become a creature of flesh and blood.

Even more remarkable was his interaction with hecklers. Whenever he spotted one, he would walk over and say something like, "You really gave me a hard time last week," to which the response was usually something like, "Well, you deserved it, trying to pass off all that bullshit!" Such exchanges invariably led to brief but very open dialogues, and I noticed that the lathe operators or blading mechanics he talked to would listen to what Gene said—really listen.

Suddenly, Gene was credible. He had ceased to be an ordinary useless manager and had become a creature of flesh and blood, someone whose opinions had some value. Gene was my boss, and I liked him for his warmth, honesty, and sense of humor. But I knew it had to be more than personality that won him respect in the eyes of that hard-bitten, cynical work force.

Now, years later, as I thought about those presentations to the hourly workers and about Gene's daily interactions with subordinates and peers as well, I realized that he often set up encounters in such a way that the people he met felt free to complain or argue, even to attack. Gene made himself vulnerable to people, and it was this deliberate vulnerability that seemed to draw people to him. Because he avoided defensiveness and opened himself to criticism, people were much more inclined to believe that the strength and force of his position was not merely contrived and rhetorical but real.

But there was more to it than that. By making the presentations himself, Gene took the heat for his own point of view. Had he let someone else deliver the message, he would have avoided some of the most unpleasant consequences of his position—not the business consequences, which he would have suffered in any case, but the personal consequences, the face-to-face consequences of conveying bad news. People want to confront the source of their difficulties. Gene gave them the chance, and they respected him for it.

From those presentations on, union-management relations took a sharp turn for the better, and Gene rapidly built credibility with the work force. He made important changes in Steam Turbine's work rules and gave individual employees broader, more flexible assignments. He also imposed layoffs, and he raised standards with respect to both throughput and error-free performance. With each change, Gene continued to open himself to arguments, complaints, and anger—all of which gradually diminished as results continued to improve and as Gene's vulnerability and courage continued to disarm opponents.

Combined with many other changes that reached well beyond the factory floor, the division's increased productivity powered Steam Turbine to greatly improved financial performance, and before long, Gene became an executive vice president. More important from my point of view, Gene became a role model for me—more of a role model than I realized at the time. He taught me how important it is to be a flesh-and-blood human being as well as a manager. He taught me that "soft" qualities like openness, sensitivity, and thoughtful intelligence are at least as critical to management success as "harder" qualities like charisma, aggressiveness, and always being right. Most important of all in the light of what happened at Synthetic Fuels, he taught me the value of vulnerability and the benefits of taking the heat for your own acts and policies.

What I had done in my meeting with the 15 employees at Synthetic Fuels was to repeat, in a smaller format, Gene's experience at Steam Turbine. As a result, it was a turning point not only for the division but for me as well. I went well beyond anything I had done previously in opening myself to others. On the surface, I was motivated by what I saw as a business need and didn't give much thought to how vulnerable the meeting would make me. Deep down, I think I was also motivated by

Gene's example, by an internalized picture of the soft manager succeeding in the face of hard challenges.

Being a soft manager is no job for the fainthearted. On the contrary, it takes a certain courage to be open-minded, well-informed, and responsible, to walk straight into adversity rather than seek to avoid it. Staying open to different possibilities can, of course, lead to vacillation, but it can also lead to tougher, better decisions from among a wider range of choices. The object of soft management is certainly not to be lax or indecisive.

People who like absolute control can't stand to see me risk my dignity and authority by opening up to others.

By the same token, whenever I'm tempted to insulate myself from the painful emotional consequences of some business decision, Gene's experience reminds me that it's more productive to listen to objections and complaints, to understand what subordinates are thinking and feeling, to open up to their arguments and their displeasure. It was this kind of vulnerability that made Gene credible to the people whose help he most needed in order to succeed.

Unfortunately, openness and vulnerability are anathema to some people. I have worked with at least two men who found my management style upsetting. Both were supremely self-confident, bright, and articulate, the kind of men who take complete charge of situations and of other human beings. I'm sure it's very uncomfortable (at an unconscious level, perhaps even frightening) for people who like to feel they are in absolute control of their surroundings to see someone like me stand so close to what they must experience as a precipice of indignity and lost authority.

In any case, they didn't like me, and I didn't like them. I believe they saw my vulnerability as exactly what they wanted to be rid of in themselves. I know I saw their exaggerated self-assurance as arrogance and insensitivity, which I wanted no part of in myself.

My position on soft management comes down to this: proponents of all management styles will probably agree that to manage other people effectively, a person needs a battery of qualities that are not easily acquired, and that these include intelligence, energy, confidence, and responsibility. Where I differ from a lot of my colleagues is in believing that candor, sensitivity, and a certain willingness to suffer the painful consequences of unpopular decisions belong on the list of necessary characteristics. Being vulnerable to the give-and-take of ordinary emotional crossfire and intellectual disagreement makes us more human, more credible, and more open to change.

Originally published in November–December 1991
Reprint 91609

Leadership in a Combat Zone

WILLIAM G. PAGONIS

Executive Summary

LIEUTENANT GENERAL WILLIAM G. PAGONIS led the 40,000 men and women who ran the theater logistics in the Persian Gulf War during its three phases of operation: Desert Shield (buildup), Desert Storm (ground war), and Desert Farewell (redeployment). By military standards, it was a challenging assignment. By the conventions of any nonmilitary complex organization, it was unheard of.

In the Persian Gulf, Pagonis's challenges included feeding, clothing, sheltering, and arming over 550,000 people. All of this in an hostile, desert region with a Muslim community distrustful of the "infidels" sent there to protect them. The lessons of leadership gleaned through Pagonis's experiences in the Gulf cross military boundaries—they apply equally to general management and leadership development in the private, civilian sector.

To gain a clear sense of the overall organization in an area the size of the Southwest Asian theater, Pagonis deputized proxies, dubbed "Ghostbusters," to be his eyes and ears throughout the desert. His goal was to build a leadership-supporting environment, combining centralized control with decentralized execution. Pagonis believes vision is defined by the leader, but the subordinates define the objectives that move the organization toward the desired outcome.

The roots of leadership, Pagonis claims, are expertise and empathy. A leader's work is not only to apply these traits but also to cultivate them—both on a personal and organizational level. True leaders create organizations that themselves cultivate leadership. This can only be achieved through rigorous and systematic organizational development.

Lieutenant General William G. Pagonis led the 40,000 men and women who ran the theater logistics for the Persian Gulf War during its three phases of operation: Desert Shield (buildup), Desert Storm (ground war), and Desert Farewell (redeployment). By military standards, it was a challenging assignment. By the conventions of any non-military, complex organization, it was unheard of. Over the course of a few hectic months, his organization, the 22nd Support Command, grew from 5 people to 40,000. The team fed, clothed, sheltered, and armed over 550,000 people. They served 122 million meals. Within the theater, they transported and distributed more than 7 million tons of supplies, 117,000 wheeled vehicles, 2,200 tracked vehicles, and 2,000 helicopters. They pumped 1.3 billion gallons of fuel. They successfully supported General

Norman Schwarzkopf's "end run" strategy, and did so in a harsh environment with almost no preexisting military infrastructure.

The 22nd Support Command's accomplishments are testimony to an often maligned branch of the Army. Logistics, at best, has been traditionally dismissed as mundane. But the lessons of leadership gleaned through Pagonis's experience in the Gulf cross military boundaries—they apply equally to general management and leadership development in the private, civilian sector.

Lt. General Pagonis is author (with Jeffrey L. Cruikshank) of Moving Mountains: Lessons in Leadership and Logistics from the Gulf War *(Harvard Business School Press, 1992).*

It has been a year and a half since I completed my tour of duty in Saudi Arabia as head of the United States Army's 22nd Support Command. And in the wake of the Allied victory over Iraq, I've read and thought a lot about my logistics profession. But I've also done a great deal of thinking about the goals, qualities, and prerequisites of leadership. And based on that reflection, I've reached a number of conclusions.

For one, I've concluded that leadership is only possible where the ground has been prepared in advance. To a certain extent, I'll be the first to admit, this process of ground-breaking is beyond the control of a lone individual in a large organization. If the organization isn't pulling for you, you're likely to be hobbled from the start. Fortunately for me and for thousands of other officers like me, the Army goes to great lengths—greater, I would argue, than any other organization—to groom and develop its leaders. Like my peers in the general officer ranks, I have been formally educated, informally mentored, and systematically rotated through a wide variety of postings, all designed to challenge me in appropriate ways (that is, to push me without setting me up to fail) and to broaden my skills and knowledge base.

But a leader is not simply a passive vessel into which the organization pours its best intentions. To lead successfully, a person must demonstrate two active, essential, and interrelated traits: expertise and empathy. In my experience, both of these traits can be deliberately and systematically cultivated; this personal development is the first important building block of leadership.

A true leader must demonstrate two active, essential, and interrelated traits: expertise and empathy.

The leadership equation has another vital piece as well. Leaders are not only shaped by the environment; they also take active roles in remaking that environment in productive ways. In other words, true leaders create organizations that support the exercise and cultivation of leadership. This can only be achieved through rigorous and systematic organizational development.

The work of leadership, therefore, is both personal and organizational. The bad news is that this means hard work—lots of it. The good news is that leaders are made, not born. I'm convinced that anyone who wants to work hard enough and develop these traits can lead.

Charisma, Presence, and Other Notions

No military commander would downplay the importance of personal presence in leadership. It's a vital attribute, particularly in a combat setting. Almost every combat-hardened officer can recall that fateful moment of truth when his or her command presence was first put to the test.

In my own case, that test came in 1968, during my first tour in Vietnam. My boat company had already more than proven its mettle, transporting artillery barges and supplies through intermittent sniper fire up and down the rivers of the Mekong Delta. But during the Tet Offensive of February, we were beset and besieged as never before.

Late one night, we received word that an orphanage was under attack and that we needed to transport troops to the site as quickly as possible. Leaving our artillery barges behind, we took about 30 volunteers in 6 boats and went 5 miles downriver. I wasn't told at the time, but the rest of my outfit was then ordered to follow along behind with our artillery barges in tow.

My small convoy had just landed the infantry troops near the orphanage when I got a radio call that our trailing barges were stopped dead in the water. The first barge had come under fire and "crabbed"—gone sideways in the river—and now two dozen boats were trapped behind the barge. Our battalion commander got on the air, advised us of the extreme danger upriver, and ordered us not to go back and rescue our comrades.

It was a moonlit night. From where we sat, chafing under our orders to stay put, we could look upriver and see the tracers burning across the water where the boats were stuck. They were in deep trouble. On the spur of the moment, following a time-honored military tradition, I developed "radio trouble"—that is, I turned the communications gear off—and addressed the crew of four on my small patrol boat. "We've got to go back and help," I told them, "but I don't want to force you. Anyone who doesn't want to join can stay here, no questions asked."

I'm proud to say that every one of those soldiers volunteered. We turned one of our boats around and headed upriver with tracers zinging over our heads and bullets bouncing off the sides of the boat. When we reached the crabbed barge, I could see that the man behind the steering wheel had frozen. I jumped from my boat onto the barge, and shook him back into action. In short order, we got the boat turned around and headed home again.

One leader's orders had been ignored, and another's followed. Why? Adrenaline was one contributing factor. So was loyalty: our comrades needed help immediately. But most important was my soldiers' trust in my judgment. Had I not already earned that trust and developed a command presence in a thousand undramatic settings, those soldiers would not have followed my lead. Had I not demonstrated my confidence that we could pull off the rescue, they would not have followed. My troops would have taken the sensible course and followed the radio's lead.

This same lesson applies to leaders in private industry. We are misled by the popular-culture portrayals of leaders. Movies and television have to deal in superficialities and sound bites. They have to emphasize charisma—a mysterious and seductive quality. But when they do so, they overlook the real roots of leadership.

Expertise and Empathy

I can think of no leader, military or business, who has achieved his or her position without some profound expertise. Most leaders first achieve mastery in a particular functional area, such as logistics, and eventually move into the generalist's realm.

Expertise grows out of hard work and, to some extent, luck. It's hard work that develops a skill base, and it's often luck that gives us the chance to apply that base.

Throughout my childhood, my parents ran small businesses: first a restaurant, and then a small hotel with a restaurant. Every member of the family was expected to pitch in. For my part, I scrubbed floors, waited on tables, did kitchen-prep, and helped keep the books. All through high school and college, my responsibilities expanded. I learned new things and kept my hand in old things.

After college graduation and ROTC training, I sought and won an Army commission. My first assignment was at Fort Knox, where those years of hands-on business training proved immediately useful in streamlining the unit's mail operations. On the strength of this success, I was asked to tackle the mess hall. This was even easier: I was already a minor expert in private-sector mess halls. Because I had expertise, I was successful; and because I was successful, I was identified by my superiors as a potential leader.

There are dozens of instances where I've grumbled my way through an assignment only to discover that the assignment has taught me a great deal, and that this learning is applicable in unexpected ways. Back in 1971, for example, I suffered through a stint of desk-bound research in which I was part of a team charged with analyzing LOTS (logistics-over-the-shore) vehicles. I was sure I was wasting my time, crunching numbers and drafting memos rather than leading troops.

Exactly 20 years later, I was in charge of—among several other resources—a flotilla of LOTS ships, which plied the coasts of Saudi Arabia serving as a backup for our truck convoys. Because I had been a member of the team that helped specify their design, I knew exactly how to use those vessels. I had expertise, which not only helped me do my job but also reinforced me as a leader in the eyes of my subordinates.

Owning the facts is a prerequisite to leadership. But there are millions of technocrats out there with lots of facts in their quiver and little leadership potential. In many cases, what they are missing is empathy. No one is a leader who can't put himself or herself in the other person's shoes. Empathy and expertise command respect.

I got my first inkling of this back in the 1950s, when I was a newsboy in my hometown of Charleroi, Pennsylvania. I started out at the age of nine, hawking afternoon editions of the *Charleroi Mail* on the corner of 5th and McKean. Things started going along pretty well for me there. I had regular customers, and I could shout out the headlines with the best of them: "Korean armistice signed! Read all about it!"

I soon began to notice, though, that the real market for papers was in the local bars and restaurants, rather than on quiet street cor-

Brash I was, even foolhardy. So I took a few licks, but I wouldn't back down.

ners like my own. At my little stand, I was averaging 50 copies a day. In the bars and restaurants, especially around dinner time, you could sell that many copies in two hours—and get tips, to boot.

I decided to mine this rich vein of opportunity. But the older newsboys, mostly 14 and 15 years old, dominated the commercial district, and they didn't appreciate my efforts to compete. A group of them paid me a visit, gave me a few licks, and suggested that I stick to my quiet little corner and stay out of their restaurants.

I did just that—for a little while. Then I went right back to selling papers in those crowded barrooms. Brash I was, even foolhardy; but I wasn't dumb. The opportunity was very good. And even then, I had a keen sense of justice. Why should the big kids control the best territory just because that was the way it had always been done? Even to the nine-year-old Gus Pagonis it was obvious that if you were going to do business, you'd better do it in the right place, and the big boys controlled the right place. I took a few more licks, but soon established myself as a savvy young businessman who wouldn't back down from a fight. I gained the older boys' respect and they no longer bothered me.

Years went by, and I gradually moved up in the newsboy hierarchy. Then one day I had a disturbing realization. I was now the "establishment." I was one of those big boys whom the young up-and-comers had to go up against. It seemed that I had a clear choice. I could perpetuate the cycle, or I could act in the spirit of empathy, based on my vivid recollection of what it felt like to get knocked around. I chose the latter course. At my urging, we came up with an arrangement that didn't cut too deeply into the profits of the veteran newsboys yet still gave the younger kids a chance to flex their entrepreneurial muscles. My peers went along with the plan because they knew I understood the situation from all sides. And I had earned a leader's respect from the younger kids through empathy.

Empathy was an absolutely vital quality in the context of the Gulf War. We asked ourselves constantly: What do the other people on our team need? Why do they think they need it, and how can we give it to them? The military always has its share of bendable rules. Can we find one to fit each situation?

Our hosts, the Saudi Arabian people and their government, were among the most important objects of this kind of attention. King Fahd had pledged his country's complete support and cooperation, and the Saudis delivered on that promise unstintingly. But both sides knew that the deployment of a half-million "infidels" into a strict Muslim society would be a daunting challenge.

We made our share of mistakes. Early in the most hectic phase of the Desert Shield deployment, for example, we decided to establish an Allied medical materiel command in the port city of Ad Dammam. American soldiers, male and female, reported to the site to unload boxes and crates of supplies. Unfortunately, we had no idea that the building we were moving into was located next to a particularly devout Muslim community, whose members were deeply offended by the sight of women with uncovered hair and rolled-up sleeves, working up a good sweat in the desert sun. Members of the community complained to the local religious police, and our female soldiers were soon subjected to catcalls and jeering.

Before the situation developed into a crisis, U.S. military leaders met with the appropriate Saudi religious and civil officials to get a handle on the cause of the disturbances. We soon reached a simple compromise: all U.S. military personnel would henceforth wear long-sleeved shirts in the city, and our female soldiers would keep their hair covered with their hats. It was a small concession, but one that greatly pleased the religious police responsible for enforcing the Sharia, or Islamic law.

We learned a great deal about the sensitivities of a Muslim community through these negotiations, and we applied the lessons in our subsequent dealings with the

Saudi population. We also took our learning one step
further. It was clear that our hosts were inclined to avoid
conflict with their 550,000 guests, at least until things
were approaching a crisis stage. It was our responsibility,
therefore, to anticipate their needs and avoid crises. One
day several months after the ground war ended, I realized that our two inactivated firing ranges were still lit-
tered with unexploded ordnance, and that the bedouins
would soon be traversing these areas again. We put ourselves in the shoes of the bedouins and also in the shoes
of the Saudi officials who had to protect the interests of
these desert wanderers. We cleaned up the ranges well
before the Saudi Arabians had to put pressure on us to
do so. With that we earned their continued respect and
cooperation.

Empathy also helps you know where you can draw the
line and make it stick. For example, some Saudi Arabians
disapproved of the U.S. female soldiers driving vehicles
and carrying weapons (activ-
ities in which Saudi Arabian
women do not engage). I
made it clear that from the
U.S. Army's perspective, a
soldier was a soldier, and
*Terrorist attacks were
still a possibility, and the
tragedy in Beirut
was fresh in our minds.*
that our lean logistical structure absolutely demanded
that all our soldiers be allowed to use the tools of their
trade. That line stuck.

Empathy counts for even more on the individual level.
This was brought home to me one afternoon in August
1991, some six months into Desert Farewell. A very
young private was sent to me by the military police for
disciplinary action. The facts of the incident were clear
enough. On the previous night, two MPs had demanded
to see the private's ID. He cussed them out and wound

up spending the night in jail. He arrived in my office looking remorseful and more than a little bit scared, and launched into a hurried and jumbled explanation. It was hot the night before, he said; he was tired, the MPs were picking on him, and so on. But when he finished making his excuses, he said simply, "I screwed up. I shouldn't have done it."

I made him think things through from the MPs' point of view. They had a job to do. Terrorist attacks were still a very real possibility, and the recent tragedies in Beirut and Berlin were very much in our minds. Tight security and ID checks were therefore still needed to protect the safety of everyone at the base. Then, after telling my wayward private that I would personally thank the MPs for their vigilance, I let him off the hook. He was out of my office in a flash.

Why did I bend the rules? Because empathy demanded it. This was a tough period. The war was long since over, and the vast majority of Coalition forces were already back in their home countries. But we logisticians were still there, picking up and packing up the theater. We were fighting a subtle battle against the perception that the "important" work of the war had already been accomplished, that the danger was past, that we were only mopping up after the main event. And, in fact, the weather *was* very hot—hotter than earlier in the summer when smoke from the oil fires in Kuwait had blocked out the sun. Inevitably, some tempers were wearing thin in the ranks. My young private had already learned his lesson, and he was more useful to me outside the brig than in.

The Steps of Leadership

I had the very good fortune early in my Army career to serve as an aide to a general officer in Germany. In that context, I visited most of the battalions and companies around the country. This was the military equivalent of a control experiment, in the sense that all of the commanders in the division were working on the same mission. But each of them approached his assignment a little bit differently—how he took care of his troops, how he briefed the results of his actions, how he presented himself. From company to company, and from battalion to battalion, what was really changing was leadership.

Even from my youthful and uninformed vantage point, it was obvious that some things worked and others didn't. And over time, I was able to distill the techniques of effective leadership that would work best for me. Cultivating leadership in yourself and in others should be done on both a personal and organizational level.

The first important step in the process of developing effective leadership may seem self-evident: *know yourself.* What's your expertise? What are your strengths? And, just as important, what are your weaknesses and how can you improve? Regularly scheduled self-examinations are a must for building and sustaining leadership.

Once you've assessed the raw material, you can draw up a plan that builds on your existing skills and knowledge. Take any steps necessary to sharpen those talents you already have or to compensate for ones you lack. Most leaders engage in public speaking, for example. Are you one of those rare leaders who can get away without making public appearances? Or could you benefit from some coaching in voice projection and deportment?

This kind of self-analysis allows you to be *real*—in my experience, a vital contributing factor in effective leadership. A person who is always playing to his or her weaknesses can't inspire much confidence in others. This is something to watch out for in matters large and small, since it's the cornerstone of presence. For example, I use a gentle kind of humor quite a bit. Humor helps me make contact with other people. But I only use humor because it comes naturally to me. I'm real when I use it. Those who aren't, shouldn't! In the same spirit, truly hopeless public speakers—of whom there are very few, by the way—should concentrate on grooming effective proxies.

A related challenge is to *learn how and what to communicate.* This comprises not only good speaking skills but also good listening skills and the ability to project and interpret body language. Many years ago, I set up formal systems to elicit constructive criticism from my subordinates. One of the first criticisms I got back was that I didn't listen well. This surprised me. Up to that moment, I thought my listening skills were as good as the next person's—maybe better. I poked around, asked questions, and eventually discovered that one basis for this judgment was a bad habit on my part. While listening to others, I had a tendency to sift quickly through mail or do an initial sort of my paperwork. My body language projected a lack of attention. With minor adjustments to my routine (maintaining eye contact during these meetings, relegating paperwork to later in the day), my report card improved. I also took to heart the advice of a wise commanding officer who said: "Never pass up the opportunity to remain silent." My subordinates soon began citing my listening skills as a strength rather than a weakness.

A third vital aspect of personal development relates directly to expertise: the leader has to *know the mission.* What needs to be accomplished? How can your expertise most effectively be channeled to do the job? This is an important part of the hard work I mentioned earlier. Leaders have to do their homework!

During the Gulf War, I directed my planning team to compile a binder, known within the command as the "Red Book," which was a complete and constantly updated collection of data outlining the developments of the conflict. Some four inches thick with charts and tables, it contained virtually all of the information I needed to keep abreast of our situation. While I was in transit from one theater location to another, that book was practically joined to me at the hip. General Schwarzkopf (or another general in the field or stateside) would frequently call me on the road or in the air with requests for specific information: how many tanks here, how much fuel there, how quickly can equipment be moved somewhere, and so on. I know that both my subordinates and superiors were regularly impressed with my almost magical grasp of the numbers. No magic was involved, I just studied that binder every chance I could.

When the elements of personal leadership development are in place, a leader can concentrate on building an appropriate context for leadership. Not surprisingly, this kind of organizational development depends, in large part, on a leader's ability to empower and motivate others to lead.

Moving Outward: Organizational Development

By definition, leaders don't operate in isolation. Nor do they command in the literal sense of the word, issuing a one-way stream of unilateral directives. Instead, leadership almost always involves cooperation and collaboration, activities that can occur only in a conducive context.

I am convinced that an effective leader can create such a context. My goal, as I set out to build a leadership-supporting environment, is to combine centralized control with decentralized execution.

This involves, first, extensive delegation. In a sense, this prerequisite is a logical extension of the personal awareness and development described above. A person who knows his or her expertise and the mission can find the right people to fill gaps. As a result, authority is pushed further and further down into the organization.

Delegation is only half of the story, though. The other piece involves system-building to ensure that the right information flows back up through the organization to the leader. This is a special challenge in an organization as traditionally bureaucratic as the Army. ("Staff grows, paper flows, no one knows," as the old saying has it.) But I suspect it's true for all human organizations.

Organizational development, then, includes a delicate balance of effective delegation and system-building. Over the years, I have developed a number of techniques and tools that help maintain this balance and ensure a smooth-running operation.

The first of these techniques is to *shape the vision*. Simple is better, since delegation depends on a shared understanding of the organizational goal. In the Gulf, we coined short sentences that captured the aim of our organization. These little nuggets were then aggressively disseminated. During the deployment phase, for example, you couldn't walk 20 feet within our headquarters without encountering the message, "Good logistics is combat power!" During the redeployment phase, safety was the overriding priority, and the vision became, "Not one more life!" Napkins, banners, buttons, newsletters: every possible tool was used toward building and underscoring a shared vision.

Vision must be defined by the leader. But it is the subordinates who must *define the objectives* that move the organization toward the desired outcome. "Objectives," in my lingo, are the concrete steps by which the vision will be realized. They must be specific and quantifiable. They should give subordinates the opportunity both to act and to assess the impact of their actions. For example: in my terminology, "win one for the Gipper" is a statement of vision. By contrast, "average 3.5 yards per carry on runs off tackle" is an objective articulated to advance the vision.

It's better to think through the Sunday game on Saturday than to kick the corpse on Monday.

A second key responsibility of the leader in building a leadership-supporting organization is to *educate*. On the first day a new person enters my command, I hold an orientation session to clarify my personal style, the organization of the command, our vision, and our shared objectives. Everyone needs to start off with the same information base. I specifically direct new arrivals to read my notebook of bulletins—a series of memoranda in which I have codified the key methods and tools of my command. The bulletins remain in a central location where they can be accessed by any member of the command at any time.

In addition, I regularly hold educational meetings, informally referred to as "skull sessions." These involve gathering a large group of people from many functional areas into one room and leading them through a discussion of how they would handle a range of hypothetical-but-plausible challenges. The goal, I tell them at the outset of the meeting, is to "do our Monday-morning quarterbacking on Saturday night." (In other words, better to think through the Sunday game in advance than to kick the corpse on Monday.) Through this device, my people are challenged to think in collaborative ways, to be aware of the real complexity of most situations, to become comfortable asking each other for advice and help, and, most important, to anticipate problems.

For the benefit of both the individual and the larger organization, it is vital to *give and get feedback.* Of course, every interaction with a subordinate, peer, or superior is an opportunity to do just that and should be used accordingly. But I've also found the need to implement a number of mechanisms to reinforce the feedback loop.

The organizational effectiveness (OE) session is one such tool. Once or twice a year, I take my top-level officers out of their normal routines for a one- or two-day organizational "retreat." On neutral ground, we go through role-playing exercises, take time for relaxation, and do some formal feedback exercises.

In this context, I've hit on one small innovation that helps to keep things productive. Each member of the command is asked to evaluate the person to his or her left. In doing so, the evaluator must identify three positive qualities in the person being scrutinized, as well as three areas where that person could improve his or her performance. Criticism tends to be taken more easily when it is not perceived as an attack. It was in this context, in fact, that I first learned about my bad listening skills—and, as we all know, the higher the rank, the harder to teach.

My second favored method for giving feedback has been a formal part of the Army organization for quite some time: the Evaluation Report. I put a personal twist on the ER by making it a multistep process. The conventional ER is a one-step process. After a subordinate has been in a given position for about a year, the superior officer fills out a written form rating the subordinate's performance. The problem is that the subordinate can perform below standard and never know it until a damning evaluation is filed away in the personnel files. This shortchanges everybody—the individual, the evaluator, and certainly the organization.

In my command, the ER is a two- or even three-step process. Each individual is evaluated about one or two months into his or her tenure in a position. During this meeting, the superior points out areas of the job at which the ratee is particularly accomplished and identifies other areas that need work. In the months that follow, each individual has an opportunity to develop and improve his or her skills before the final evaluation report. In the meantime, the organization benefits from improved productivity and open communication.

In complex organizations, it is important to *emphasize formal communication* with structures designed to complement the chain of command. My notebook of bulletins is one such tool. There are many others.

My work days, for example, are punctuated by a series of meetings. The first is the daily "stand-up," attended by at least one representative of each functional area in the command. (During the Gulf War, the stand-up was a chance for people to make quick status reports and then field questions.) At the end of each day, we hold a "sit-down" meeting, which gives us a chance to engage in a more concentrated kind of analysis. The sit-down also uses a "three-up, three-down" device similar to the one employed in my OE sessions. Each functional commander reports daily on three areas in his or her command that are improving and three areas that need attention.

In between these two meetings are other communications devices. For example, a few hours of my afternoon are divided into 15-minute segments called "Please See Me" time. When someone's ideas have puzzled or intrigued me, I ask them to come in and talk during one of these slots. In addition, any member of the command who has a question or a problem can sign up for a quarter-hour slot.

For straight talk, nothing compares with what I hear during my daily basketball game with the troops.

This part of the scheduling process is completely democratic. Any member of the command can sign up for a meeting, and no one ever gets bounced through rank-pulling.

And finally, there's my favorite low-tech, high-yield information transfer system: the 3 inch by 5 inch index card. I stumbled upon the 3 x 5 as a mode of communication completely by accident early in my career, and I've used it ever since. In the Gulf, questions or comments written on a 3 x 5 were guaranteed to move through the chain of command (informing appropriate personnel along the way) until they reached someone with the knowledge and authority to respond to them, and then they were returned to their authors—all within 24 hours, guaranteed. During the height of the conflict, I got about 100 a day, and every one was useful.

Formal methods of information transfer are very important, but I find that you don't get a complete view of what's actually happening in an organization unless you also open regular informal communication channels. For straight talk, nothing compares with the comments I pick up during my daily basketball game with the troops. Similarly, when my wife and I invite troops into our home for a lasagna dinner, we hope to show them that we, too, are human and approachable.

Sometimes the soldiers come to me; other times, I go to them. I devote a good deal of my time to "management by walking around." In the Gulf, MBWA took me from the frontline logbases where ammunition, food, and fuel were distributed to the troops, to the materiel dumps. I spent time with the MPs guarding the main supply routes and the "washrack" jocks responsible for cleaning and sterilizing the tanks and helicopters we were about to send home. I visited enemy prisoner-of-war camps that had been hastily erected as the ground war ended, the docks and airfields, and a hundred other more or less remote facilities.

I worked hard to be a real and constant presence throughout the desert, in all parts of the command. But the Southwest Asian theater was so large that I couldn't be in enough places often enough. Recognizing that fact, I deputized a group of soldiers—dubbed the "Ghostbusters"—as my proxies. They went into the desert as my official eyes and ears, making sure everything was running smoothly, giving and gaining a clearer sense of the theater's overall organization.

That was the point of all of this meeting, mentoring, and moving around? In a sense, it was to touch as many people, and as many kinds of people, as possible. Leaders must be motivators, educators, role models, sounding boards, confessors, and cheerleaders—they must be accessible, and they must aggressively pursue contact with colleagues and subordinates.

Muscle Memory: A Concluding Thought

Successful leadership is not mysterious. Leaders must set their own agendas and use the tools and techniques best suited to help them achieve their goals. But leadership is not entirely formulaic. Leaders must learn to trust their instincts and play their hunches.

When the fighting ended in the Gulf, an Army unit was asked to make the physical preparations for the peace talks. As the talks grew near, I developed a strange conviction—a gnawing in the pit of my stomach—that something wasn't right up in Safwan, Iraq, site of the talks. The night before the meetings were scheduled to start, I commandeered a Black Hawk helicopter to go up and take a look and discovered that the job was less than half completed. The necessary supplies had been caught in a monumental traffic jam and hadn't gotten through. Through a superhuman effort, working all night with the materials that were at hand, we made it possible for the peace talks to proceed on schedule. (I'm sure that history will record only that General Pagonis inexplicably fell asleep during the talks and slipped off his chair!)

It is said that once a basketball player practices his shots enough times, he develops a "muscle memory" of how to sink those shots. Only then is he truly free to improvise on the court. Similarly, I'm convinced that if someone works hard at leadership, his or her instincts will tend to be right. His or her hunches will be based on expertise and empathy, and they'll be good ones. Leadership will seem to come easily.

Originally published in November–December 1992
Reprint 92607

Leadership

Sad Facts and Silver Linings

THOMAS J. PETERS

Executive Summary

SENIOR MANAGERS ARE USED TO hearing advice
about how they can combat sloppiness and introduce
rationality or neatness into their decision making. In this
article, first published in 1979, Thomas Peters argues
that "sloppiness" is overwhelmingly normal, probably
inevitable, and usually sensible. For example, in the
course of a typical day, senior executives face endless
interruptions and limited options for action. Those in
charge may not even hear about choices, or any bad
news that might require action, until it's almost too late.
Furthermore, any decision that is made will probably
require months or years to implement fully. Peters suggests that these "sad facts" of managerial life can be
turned into opportunities to communicate values and to
persuade.

For instance, enough one-option choices come the leader's way that eventually he or she can shape them into a coherent portfolio that signals to the organization the leader's preferences and general strategic direction. The fragmented nature of the executive's workday can also create a succession of opportunities to tackle bits of the issue stream. The fragmentation is precisely what permits a manager to fine-tune, test, and retest the strategic signals being sent out to the company. What's more, the months or years it takes for major decisions to emerge give the leader opportunities to build consensus that will require only minimal correction over time.

Radically reimagining the senior executive's role, Peters suggests that the leader's task is not to impose an abstract order on an inherently disorderly process. Instead, the leader must become adept at controlling the process by nudging it in the desired direction.

It may come as some consolation to frazzled executives that there have never been enough hours in the working day. Business was already moving at blistering speed when this article first appeared in 1979. And as far back as 1955, Fortune *magazine wrote of the typical senior executive, "He [authors always assumed a "he" in those days] is constantly pressed for time."*

The speed of business is the enemy of tidy rationality. Urgent phone calls interrupt long-planned meetings, noisy problems break into time allotted to quiet reflection, and before long, the orderly world of the executive's schedule is in shambles.

Which is just fine, says author Tom Peters, in 1979 a consultant at McKinsey & Company but soon to go on to fame as coauthor of In Search of Excellence. *The leader's job is not to defend a rigid timetable against reality but to promote and protect the organization's values. Interruptions offer an opportunity to do so. A crisis with a key client may force you to cut short a product development meeting. Perfect— a chance to demonstrate how to solve problems and care for customers. In other words, you know you've had a good day when nothing goes according to plan.*

YOU ARE EXECUTIVE VICE PRESIDENT of a sizable corporation, challenged by competitors at home and abroad. During the past year, you have tried to get the organization moving on a much-needed overhaul of the product line. Today one of the task forces will spend all day reviewing its key findings with you.

Twenty minutes into the presentation, it is already clear that the task force has come up with a future product array with no apparent flexibility. You are being asked to bet several million dollars on a risky slate that is sure to be challenged before the first products hit the marketplace.

Then at 9:35 you are pulled out of the review to talk with the vice chairman about a product safety challenge that has just hit the local press. You get back to the meeting at 11:05, only to be pulled out again at 11:40: The president wants to verify the amount of capital spending in next year's budget before a luncheon with an outside board member. Finally, after returning at 12:35, you are pulled out for good at 2:15 to meet a major customer who has flown in unexpectedly to talk about a $20 million bid that one of your major divisions just made. So, in the end, the six straight hours you had planned to give to that all-important product-line issue were cut down to less than three.

The preceding situation would expose you to attack from two kinds of management thinkers. Decision-making theorists would chide you for failing to develop a wide range of options. Time-effectiveness experts would criticize you for not going off campus and devoting the full six-hour block to such a major issue.

There is, however, another side to the coin: The scenario just sketched is typical of the real world of senior management; it is, in fact, the norm.

Executives have sensed for years that this series of interruptions with the task at hand sandwiched in represents a true picture of the way they do business, but only recently has such a routine been thoroughly documented. Canadian researcher Henry Mintzberg noted in an article ("The Manager's Job: Folklore and Fact," HBR July–August 1975) that they moved in a fragmented fashion through a bewildering array of issues on any given day; in fact, fully half of their activities were completed in less than nine minutes.

Moreover, he argued that such behavior was probably both appropriate and efficient. A chief executive officer provides a unique perspective and is a unique information source, Mintzberg pointed out. His ability to influence a large number of activities through brief contacts may, in fact, be a highly leveraged use of his time. More recently, examining 25 major business decisions, Mintzberg found that, in every case, top management deliberation focused on only one option. They were all go/no-go issues—not a multiple choice question in the lot.

More than a decade ago, H. Edward Wrapp postulated in a much-quoted article ("Good Managers Don't Make Policy Decisions," HBR September–October 1967) that the successful manager "recognizes the futility of trying to push total packages or programs through the organization. . . . Avoiding debates on principles, he tries to piece together particles that may appear to be incidentals into a program that moves at least part way toward [his goals]."

Without offering many prescriptions, other researchers, too, are challenging the conventional organizational wisdom concerning the supposed advantages of orderly decision-making processes and the supposed waste of time of meetings, telephone conversations, unscheduled interruptions, and so on. The researchers do not deny the *rationality* of accepted notions about how a top executive ought to spend his time, nor do they dismiss out of hand the values of orderly management.

Rather, by challenging the realism of advice based on a model so much less messy than the real world, they suggest that executive behavior that results from an ad hoc adaptation to shifting circumstances is not in itself irrational. Such behavior might, after all, prove to be the expression of a very different organizing principle.

Reckoning with Realities

Over the past two years, several of my colleagues and I have been attempting to analyze the workings of advanced decision-making systems in some two dozen corporations in the United States and Western Europe. In general, our observations support the views of the realists against the less practical rationalizations of conventional organization theory. Our findings can be summarized under the following four headings:

1. **Senior managers will usually receive for review what amounts to a single option (one new product**

slate, one acquisition candidate, one major investment proposal) rather than a set of fully developed
choices. They usually face yes-or-no decisions rather
than trade-offs. Rarely, moreover, does the proposal
that they see include assessments of possible competitive responses or government constraints that
are likely to emerge over the long term.

2. **Senior management will spend most of its time
fighting fires and may not come upon critical
issues until late in the game.** It is unusual for senior
management to get a look at proposals when the
options are still wide open. Published scientific
papers (the equivalent of polished proposals) typically suggest an "immaculate, rational, step-by-step
approach to discovery," notes science historian
Robert Merton in his book *Social Theory and Social
Structure* (Free Press, 1968); the dead ends and
assumptions left untested because of time constraints never show up in the finished product.

3. **Senior managers will be shielded from most bad
news.** Obviously, the monthly or quarterly revenues
and net income figures that top managers see are
reasonably straightforward and timely; even by playing with receivables or speeding up deliveries, a division manager cannot hide bad news at this level for
long. But *really* bad news—for example, on a share
decline in a critical segment of a product line—can
be concealed for months, sometimes for years.

4. **Most really important decisions emerge only after
top managers have vacillated for months or years,
and the solution they choose at the end may well
be indistinguishable from that proposed at the
beginning of the search.** In practice, top managers

typically respond to major issues with trial balloons. They seldom make a public commitment to a choice before they are quite sure that: (a) its wisdom is no longer open to serious question, and (b) the organization is agreeable.

Each of these observations seemingly casts a gloomy cloud over the potential for a rational organization theory. Yet I would argue that each can have a silver lining. The purpose of this article is to point out these silver linings and to suggest how senior executives can take advantage of them.

First, however, an important preliminary point: The four observations appear to be as characteristic of companies that perform well as of those that perform poorly. They are not, in other words, symptoms of some sort of organizational malaise that should be (or could be) "put right."

At first glance, the four observations offer no obvious encouragement to the senior executive who aspires to shape events and to leave a mark of excellence behind. Considered more thoughtfully, however, they do suggest a hopeful hypothesis: *Perhaps* the seemingly disorderly bits of the choice process make available to the senior executive a set of opportunities to impart a thrust to, or to fine-tune, his organization's sense of direction. I believe that this is indeed the case. Let us examine each observation in turn and try to discover its potential silver lining. (See the exhibit "Real-World Decision Making.")

Not Enough Choices

Sad Fact No. 1: Senior managers get only one option.

Silver Lining: (a) The option is in accord with senior managers' preferences; (b) there are enough one-option choices in a given period to permit managers to shape them, over time, as a portfolio.

There is nothing wrong with one option if it is an option the senior manager wants to see. This is an obvious statement, perhaps, but it has not-so-obvious impli-

---

Real-World Decision Making: Ragged but Right

Not Enough Choices
Sad Fact No. 1

Silver Lining

Senior managers get only one option.	• The option usually reflects senior leaders' previously expressed preferences.
	• Leaders eventually get enough one-option choices to shape them into a coherent portfolio.

Not Enough Time
Sad Fact No. 2

Time is fragmented; issues arrive late, fully staffed.	• Each fragment can be used to signal leaders' preferences and set direction.
	• Small, last-minute modifications of current options strongly signal what future options should look like.

Too Many Filters
Sad Fact No. 3

Bad news is normally hidden.	• Senior leaders can use their responses to good news to reinforce the organization's values and priorities.

Too Much Inertia
Sad Fact No. 4

Major choices take months or years to emerge.	• Over time, consistent choices accumulate into a consensus that requires minimal correction. And with a large number of choices in the hopper, decisions will come frequently enough to spell out leaders' chosen direction.

cations. First, it assumes that the senior manager's main business is unearthing concerns, reminding people about past errors, setting directions, and building management capabilities. Chief executives have little enough time to spend "on the issues"—too little to spend it making complex trade-offs between action alternatives. Their real question, then, is less likely to be "Where are the other options?" than "Does this option contain the thrust we want to see?"

Suppose top managers are worried that their company is making a relatively high-cost product in a major line; it is making Oldsmobiles for a Chevrolet (or Honda) market. The new product slate comes up. Broadly, they want to know: Is it a low-cost slate? More important, is it *different* from the slates of past years—different in the way they want to see? Top managers' yes-or-no decision on the proposal is not a check on its optimality. It is, however, a check on its direction and a signal back to, say, division management that "we think you have (or have not) gotten the message."

Next, consider this one-option agenda over six months or so. There may be a half-dozen decisions of note, which add up to a reasonably sizable portfolio of choices. Viewed in this light, the quarterly or annual slate of choices becomes an array of opportunities to communicate, reinforce, or adjust in a direction top management wishes to pursue.

Not Enough Time

Sad Fact No. 2: Time is fragmented; issues arrive late, fully staffed.

Silver Lining: (a) Each fragment can be used to convey preferences so that the calendar or agenda as a whole provides an opportunity to set direction; (b) lateness is relative; each slight modification of the current option becomes a strong signal about what the next one should look like.

The point here is that fragmentation can, if properly managed, be a positive advantage. As Richard Neustadt wrote of Franklin Roosevelt:

"He had a strong feel for the cardinal fact of government: that presidents don't act on policies, programs or personnel in the abstract; they act in the concrete as they meet deadlines set by due dates, act on documents awaiting signatures, vacant posts awaiting appointees, officials seeking interviews, newsmen seeking answers, audiences waiting for a speech, etc."[1]

The fragments that compose the executive's working day can be used as a succession of opportunities to tackle bits of the issue stream. It is precisely the fragmented nature of their activity that permits top managers to fine-tune, test, and retest the general strategic direction they are trying to impart to their companies over the longer term.

Moreover, fragmentation of time, properly exploited, can yield a rich variety of information. Within reason, the more views and visits in the top executive's schedule and the more numerous the interruptions and unscheduled encounters, the better informed he is likely to be. As Mintzberg observes, "The chief executive tolerates interruption because he does not wish to discourage the flow of current information."[2]

The potential danger is equally clear: The fragmentation of his time multiplies opportunities for the executive to send inconsistent signals to the organization. To send effective signals to, say, the 25 to 75 key executives in an organization, the top management team must obviously be clear on the general message it wants to get across.

The second aspect of this fact of life is late exposure to issues. Senior managers must accept their fate as reviewers of completed staff work. Rarely does a rough draft, rife with contention over key assumptions or problem attributes, reach the executive suite.

Again, fragmentation, employed effectively, can provide a partial answer. By their very position, top managers seldom deal with problems in isolation. They deal with a flow. Each brief exposure to an issue becomes an opportunity to express general concerns and to gradually sharpen the responses of the organization to reflect the same concerns. One CEO, in the midst of a strategic crisis, devoted a lot of time to a seemingly insignificant customer complaint because, as he explained afterward, it gave him a chance to demonstrate an approach to broad competitive issues that he was trying to instill throughout the organization.

Too Many Filters

Sad Fact No. 3: Bad news is normally hidden.

Silver Lining: Review and comment on details of good news offer a chance to shape attitudes and preferences so that those down the line will share senior management's priorities.

Inevitably, most news sent up the line to senior managers will be "good"; and, in any case, the chief executive is too far removed from daily operations to unerringly ask the crucial question that might open up a Pandora's box. True, he can take advantage of the fragmentation of his time to tap multiple sources of information and catch, by designed chance, a few reviews and analyses while debate is still focused on objectives and assumptions rather than on how to package a chosen option so that the "old man" (or the finance staff) will buy it.

More important, however, is the opportunity that the good news presents. Much can be accomplished through a style of good-news review that zeroes in on almost any sort of significant subpoint for special attention and comment. In dealing with the problem of how overextended and partially ignorant congressmen can quickly inform themselves on complex issues, political scientist Aaron Wildavsky makes a relevant point:

"Another way of handling complexity is to use actions on simpler items as indices of more complicated ones. Instead of dealing with the cost of a huge atomic installation, congressmen may seek to discover how personnel and administrative costs or real estate transactions with which they have some familiarity are handled. The reader has probably heard of this practice under some such title as 'straining at gnats.' This practice may at times have greater validity than appears on the surface if it is used as a testing device, and if there is a reasonable connection between the competence shown in handling simple and complex items."[3]

Top managers regularly use forays into detail as a shield against surprise, and, over time, they can learn a lot this way. More important, though, such attention conveys a sense of "how we deal with problems" and indicates the sort of understanding of issues that is expected of managers down the line. If, additionally, top managers' probings clearly reflect concern with a particular issue, the danger that their subordinates will lose sight of that issue will be slight.

Such irregular involvement with detail contrasts markedly with the exclusive use of staff for probing. Obviously, staff probes can be productive in some situations, but in others they may simply drive the bad news further into hiding. While using his staff as merciless probers, ITT's legendary chief executive Harold Geneen was a firm believer in face-to-face reviews because, as he put it, "You can tell by the tone of voice if a fellow is having a problem he hasn't reported yet."

A simple but often overlooked aspect of good-news review is the use of praise. An executive can use detailed good-news review deliberately to reinforce desired patterns of action or response. One CEO, when attending field reviews, always stopped in at a regional sales office or plant. He would dig into the records ahead of time, pick out an exemplary action by some salesman or foreman, and make a point of asking him how he had done this or that so well.

He might then take up the idea in a memo that would be sent all around the company. Again, if in the course of a presentation a junior staff man came up with a particularly clever analysis that fit in well with the CEO's current main concern—for example, looking at the competitor's position in a new way—he would interrupt the presentation and raise the possibility of introducing the idea into a large class of proposals or reviews.

Too Much Inertia

Sad Fact No. 4: Major choices take months or years to emerge.

Silver Lining: The process of choosing provides an opportunity to build a strong consensus for consistently implementing actions that will require only minimal correction over time. If enough choices are in the hopper, the lengthy sorting process will be punctuated by fairly frequent decisions that will support (or serve to test) top managers' chosen directions.

An instructive case in point concerns a large industrial products company, long dominated by engineers, that found itself threatened in frightening new ways. Overseas competitors' products were nicking sizable chunks from previously uncontested market segments. Cash-rich domestic competitors were investing in small companies making promising substitute products for some key lines. The threat was both diffuse and pervasive.

Gradually, over a three- to five-year period, the top team became convinced that its main task was to instill a marketing orientation. Early steps, all in the nature of trial balloons, included: (1) going outside to hire three senior marketers from companies with outstanding marketing reputations; (2) creating a top-level task force to assess the five-year competitive outlook; and (3) giving one of the new marketers a special new product group with a sizable budget to develop a product slate for one of the threatened market niches.

Approximately 18 months later, some more definite signals came of what was afoot: a major speech to security analysts outlining the company's new approach to marketing; irregular visits to important customers by the president and top team; the establishment of a monthly president's review, marked by several special sessions on competitive assessment and the beginning of share reporting in certain businesses; the creation of a large number of new assistant regional sales manager jobs and the hiring of highly paid MBAs to fill them. Finally, at about the three-year mark, the top team took some very conspicuous actions. It promoted two of the three marketers who had been recruited on the outside, together with two insiders, to the position of senior vice president, with realigned market responsibilities.

At the annual shareholders meeting the top team launched a new theme: "Our emerging role is to be preeminent in marketing." It brought out a slate of surprisingly good new products, striking back hard at competitors in one or two besieged market segments. Internally, it publicly introduced a new management-information and cost system that had been implemented after three years of gradual, incremental development.

Thus, over a 36-month period, without much fanfare, the top team successfully shifted the institution's attention to the marketplace. Observers today, while noting that engineers still win a fair share of their battles, agree that the company has undergone a radical transformation.

Developing a top management consensus in favor of such a major shift can be a delicate and time-consuming business. Bringing along one crucial member of a triumvirate (or at least effectively neutralizing his opposition) can take years. During such a process, even a decision about when to send up the next trial balloon may be politically loaded. As Peter Drucker wisely noted, "Priorities are easy; posteriorities—what jobs *not* to tackle—are tough." His point is consistent with a wide body of psychological research on building commitment and overcoming resistance to change: Keeping a dissident actor from quick-triggering with a negative response is no easy chore.

The period of muddling about on the way to major change is not purely a matter of political maneuvering. At least as important is the "marinating time" it provides. In one company I know, the top 12 executives met weekly for several hours, over an 18-month period, in order to draft a modified change of charter for the company. They have used the resulting document, which they call their "Magna Carta," as the jumping-off point for a decade of substantial positive change. It is only two pages long. But it took this management group nearly two years to work through the critical issues involved and to come to terms with the new departures involved, although they had had a fairly good idea from the beginning what the shape of the outcome would be.

The period of muddling about on the way to major change is not purely a matter of political maneuvering. At least as important is the "marinating time" it provides.

Revamping Management's Role

Each of the four seemingly discouraging facts of executive life can, as we have seen, be recast in positive terms. The results add up to a fresh conception of the top management task, one that fits both the disorderly facts of life and their recurrent silver linings. It rejects the traditional notion of the executive as dedicating large, discrete blocks of time to linear chunks called "planning," "deciding," or "implementing" and replaces it with something closer to a notion of the effective executive as a communicator, a persuader, and above all, a consummate opportunist. He is adept at grasping and taking advantage of each item in the random succession of time and issue fragments that crowd his day.

This reconception of the top management task requires hard thinking about what is and what is not achievable from the top. The CEO does not drive forklifts or install phones; management theory has long acknowledged that limitation. Research is beginning to suggest a further off-limits area—top managers cannot *solve* problems: Their attention is fragmented; issues come to them late; and they are shielded from bad news. What they can do is: (1) generally shape business values, and (2) educate by example.

Shaping Business Values

In his landmark study of top management activity, Philip Selznick concludes that the effective institutional leader "is primarily an expert in the promotion and protection of values."[4] Another recent study of leadership by James McGregor Burns contrasts lesser forms of management behavior with "transforming leadership," which, in the midst of the disorderly press of events, unleashes organizational energies through the promotion of new, overarching values.[5]

The same theme is echoed by Roy Ash, who created new institutional forms at Litton Industries and the U.S. Office of Management and Budget and is currently in the process of reviving Addressograph-Multigraph. As he sees it, the really important change in a company lies in a process of "psychological transformation." One of Ash's recent notes to himself, as quoted in *Fortune,* clarifies his meaning. It reads, "Develop a much greater attachment of everybody to the bottom line—more agony and ecstasy."[6]

As descriptions of the top management task, these terms—institutional leadership, value promotion, transforming leadership—are surprisingly congenial to the disorderly, nonrational realities of most real-life management activity. In an untidy world, where goal setting, option selection, and policy implementation hopelessly fuzz together, the shaping of robust institutional values through a principle of ad hoc opportunism becomes preeminently the mission of the chief executive and his most senior colleagues.

The nature of this value-shaping process is not obvious. Among a group of chief executives (actually mayors) they studied, John Kotter and Paul Lawrence found that the more successful executives typically spent over a year carefully taking the pulse of key stakeholders, seeding ideas, and nursing along a consensus in favor of a few new directions. The less effective executives were those who plunged into major commitments before they had built adequate support.[7]

My own observations are wholly consistent with those of Kotter and Lawrence. The process of easing a larger organization into a major shift of values seems to require anywhere from three to eight years. A good example is the experience of Walter Spencer of Sherwin-Williams, who spent his first five years as CEO working to introduce a marketing orientation into a previously manufacturing-dominated institution. "When you take a 100-year-old company and change the culture of the organization, and try to do that in Cleveland's traditional business setting—well, it takes time; you just have to keep hammering at everybody," Spencer told an interviewer from *Forbes.* "The change over to marketing is probably irreversible now. It's not complete, but we've brought along a lot of young managers with that philosophy, and once you've taken a company this far, you can't go back."[8]

The literature of top management generally ignores the intricacies of effective value management, especially the aspect of timing. Yet almost any chief executive knows how much time he must spend on patiently building support for his initiatives. Only when crisis is imminent can the process be condensed, and even then some form of consensus building is needed.

The art of value management, then, blends strategic foresight with a shrewd sense of timing and the political acumen necessary to build stable, workable coalitions. Fortunately, the practical exercise of these skills—as opposed to the textbook fantasies of rational problem solving—is actually enhanced by the untidiness of typical executive choice processes.

CEO as Exemplar

Top management's actions, over time, constitute the guiding, directing, and signaling process that shapes values in the near chaos of day-to-day operations. As Eli Ginzberg and Ewing Reilley have noted: "Those a few echelons from the top are always alert to the chief executive. Although they attach much importance to what he says, they will be truly impressed only by what he does."[9] Top management is at the apex of the symbolic signaling system, not the hard product-delivery system. Because senior managers cannot act directly or promptly to resolve issues, their daily efforts must focus on sending effective and appropriate signals. Recounts one chief executive:

"The board's question at my first meeting was trivial: Could I get them speedier information about the installation of new machines? I used the situation as a simple teaching opportunity. I responded with the data requested but recast it in market-share terms. My intent was to wean them away from thinking that the gross number was still an adequate measure of health. That little incident was my first easy opportunity to expose them to share issues."

The executive who sees his role in these terms is aware that symbol management is a source of both unparalleled opportunity and, for the unwary, unparalleled risk. Knowing that subordinates will eventually make detailed interpretations of his every activity ("The boss was huddling with the investment bankers, was he?" the subordinate might ask himself. "Maybe he wants to unload my division"), he will be scrupulously careful to avoid distracting signals. "People keep searching for clues," notes linguist Julius Roth. "The poorer and fewer the clues, the more desperate the search."[10]

Several business scholars and political scientists have suggested the image of the "leader as educator." Such a leader, in Selznick's words, must be able to "interpret the role of the enterprise, to perceive and develop models of thought and behavior, and to find general, rather than merely partial, perspectives."[11]

Beyond that, he needs to be able to articulate his vision in a compelling way. Warren Bennis underscores the point: "If I were to give off-the-cuff advice to anyone trying to institute change, I would say, 'How clear is the metaphor? How is that understood? How much energy are you devoting to it?' It's the imagery that creates the understanding, the compelling moral necessity that the new way is right. It was the beautiful writing of Darwin about his travels on the *Beagle,* rather than the content of his writing, that made the difference. The evolutionary idea had really been in the air for quite a while."[12]

If it is in shaping values that the senior executive can most efficiently use his time, it is symbols that are his primary value-shaping tools. As an educator, he has quite an arsenal of pedagogical tricks of the trade at his disposal: manipulation of settings, varied repetition of signals, a range of sensitive responses to subtle feedback cues. Consider:

- Careful use of language, including insistently asked questions and attention to the minutiae of written proposals.

- Manipulation of settings, including the creation of forums and rules of debate designed to focus on critical concerns.

- Shifts of agenda and time allocation to signal, subtly but pervasively, a change in priorities.

- Consistent and frequent feedback and reinforcement, including the careful and selective interpretation of past results to stress a chosen theme.

- Selective seeding of ideas among various internal power groups and cultivation of those that win support.

Collectively, these enable the CEO to intervene purposefully and effectively in what one philosopher called "the brute flow of random detail that adds up to everyday experience."

Concluding Note

Senior managers are used to hearing and reading advice about how they can combat sloppiness and introduce rationality or neatness into decision making. I have argued that "sloppiness" is normal, probably inevitable, and usually sensible. Organizations in the process of making important choices almost always look disorderly. But that apparent disorder can provide the latitude and the time required for the development of consensus; and without consensus, efforts at implementation will be doomed from the start.

The task of the senior executive, then, is not to impose an abstract order on an inherently disorderly process but to become adept at the sorts of intervention by which he can nudge it in the desired direction and control its course.

Notes

1. Richard E. Neustadt, "Approaches to Staffing the Presidency," *American Political Science Review,* December 1963.

2. Henry Mintzberg, *The Nature of Managerial Work* (Harper & Row, 1973).

3. Aaron Wildavsky, *The Politics of the Budgetary Process* (Little, Brown, 1964).

4. Philip Selznick, *Leadership in Administration* (Row, Peterson, 1957).

5. James McGregor Burns, *Leadership* (Harper & Row, 1978).

6. Louis Kraar, "Roy Ash Is Having Fun at Addressogrief-Multigrief," *Fortune,* February 27, 1978.

7. John P. Kotter and Paul R. Lawrence, *Mayors in Action* (John Wiley and Sons, 1974).

8. Harold Seneker, "Why Some CEOs Pop Pills (and Sometimes Quit)," *Forbes,* July 12, 1978.

9. Eli Ginzberg and Ewing W. Reilley, *Effecting Change in Large Organizations* (Columbia University Press, 1957).

10. Julius A. Roth, *Timetables* (Bobbs-Merrill, 1963).

11. Selznick.

12. Warren Bennis, *The Unconscious Conspiracy: Why Leaders Can't Lead* (AMACOM, 1976).

Originally published in December 2001
Reprint R0111J

The Leadership Lessons of Mount Everest

MICHAEL USEEM

Executive Summary

THE HIMALAYAS ARE one of nature's most demanding classrooms, but they can teach us important principles about taking charge of our followers—and our own egos. In this article, Wharton professor Michael Useem recounts the experiences of MBA graduates and mid-career executives who took part in a leadership program on the lower slopes of Mount Everest. Conceived to heighten participants' appreciation of what leadership is all about, the program transforms abstract concepts into practice: Not only do people learn from the historical expeditions of others, they also gain insights from their own unfolding experiences.

Through hiking some 80 miles over rough terrain, the participants learned about their own limitations—one CEO grappled with the decision to turn back when others feared the altitude had become too much for him—

and about the value of communication—what to do when several team members are unaccounted for as night falls. The team also learned from those they met along the path to Everest's base camp. They benefited from rare encounters such as a private audience with the reincarnate lama, the spiritual leader for the region's largely Buddhist population and a discussion with a passing hiker who had been part of the harrowing Everest expedition described in the best-seller *Into Thin Air*.

During the journey, four essential principles emerged: Leaders should be led by the group's needs; inaction can sometimes be the most difficult—but wisest—action; if your words don't stick, you haven't spoken; and leading upward can feel wrong even when it's right.

Through compelling stories of the trekkers' triumphs and miscalculations, the author sheds new light on several central management principles.

Our twin otter was descending at a dangerously steep angle, but at the last minute the pilot managed to pull the nose up and ease us onto the runway. We had arrived at the gateway to the Himalayas—a tiny airstrip surrounded by snow-covered peaks in the village of Lukla, elevation 9,350 feet. With fully laden backpacks and a keen sense of adventure, we began our journey into the mountain range capped by Mount Everest.

We went to the Himalayas to learn about leadership in one of the outdoors' most stunning yet demanding classrooms. For the next 11 days, our team of 20 trekkers, including MBA graduates and midcareer executives, hiked some 80 miles over rough terrain to reach a high point of over 18,000 feet. Through our experiences along the way, we heightened our understanding of what true leadership is all about.

Of course, we didn't need to travel halfway around the world to appreciate the basic principles of leadership. All of us already recognized that leadership requires strategic thinking, decisive action, personal integrity, and other worthy qualities. Yet we also knew that converting such abstract concepts into practice is often an elusive process. Indeed, few behavioral concepts defy translation into reality as much as those that involve leadership.

We made the trip to Mount Everest not because it could teach us things about leadership that we couldn't have learned elsewhere but because the lessons there would have a far greater urgency. When problems arose, they could rapidly worsen—or be resolved—depending on how quickly people put into action those theoretical leadership concepts. For the hundreds of trekkers who have attempted to reach the summit of Mount Everest, effective leadership has often literally meant the difference between life and death.

For us, hiking along the lower slopes, the decisions we would make would not have the same life-or-death consequences. Nevertheless, our journey would push us in untold ways. Most people in our group had no mountaineering experience whatsoever; many had never spent a single night camping in a tent. So hiking ten miles a day over tough landscape at high altitudes would test people as they had never been tested before. And although we planned to stay along the lower ridges of Mount Everest, we were well aware of the dangers of altitude sickness and careless mistakes—a bad slip could result in a sprained or broken ankle, a minor disaster in such a remote location.

With our senses heightened to such risks, we would be more receptive to the leadership lessons we would learn. Specifically, over the course of our journey, four essential principles emerged: Leaders should be led by the group's needs; inaction can sometimes be the most difficult—but wisest—action; if your words don't stick, you haven't spoken; and leading upwards can feel wrong when it's right.

From Gettysburg to Everest

Before we look at the lessons in more detail, first a word about the genesis of the Mount Everest program. The impetus for the expeditions dates to the early 1990s. At the time, recruiters from investment banks, consulting firms, and other companies said that they liked the functional skills of Wharton graduates, but they also wanted those newly minted managers to be able to lead. Their markets were far too unpredictable and fast moving for anything less. But teaching leadership in the classroom was one thing; actually implementing those skills in the workplace was quite another.

To help fill that gap, I began creating off-site experiences intended to enhance our graduates' understanding of leadership. The first was a one-day program in which our executive MBA students walked the Gettysburg battlefield and discussed the leadership lessons of that pivotal struggle more than a century ago. The Himalayas presented another, more powerful venue for the same kind of inductive learning. Not only could participants benefit from the historical expeditions of others, they could also learn from their own unfolding experiences.

So four years ago, my associate Edwin Bernbaum, the director of the Sacred Mountains Program at the Mountain Institute, and I launched an annual program that is open to our MBA and executive MBA graduates, as well as to managers who have completed one of our executive programs. Each participant can bring along a guest, perhaps a spouse or coworker, with the proviso that everyone is a student and must take part in all activities. A typical group consists of some 20 men and women, ranging in age from their 20s to their 50s. For months before arriving in Nepal, participants work themselves into the best physical shape possible, exercising aerobically five or six days a week, often on a hilly trail, a treadmill, or StairMaster. Some have even hired personal trainers to prepare for the journey.

During the treks (this article draws on four of them), we explored the leadership terrain through three methods that continually reinforced one another, often in unexpected ways. First, we held daily seminars over lunch and dinner, drawing on preassigned materials, including books, articles, and cases of the past triumphs and disasters of mountaineers who have attempted to reach the Himalayas' uppermost ridges. Second, every day two participants took their turn as leaders, assuming responsibility for the day's hiking assignments, logistical issues, and seminar topics. The day leaders also handled personnel problems ranging from irritation to illness. Each night, the entire group held a discussion to learn from everyone's experiences, analyzing the tribulations we had faced and miscalculations we had made. Third, as we hiked the path toward the base camp of Mount Everest, we encountered climbers who just days earlier had themselves been on its highest slopes or even its summit. We learned from their firsthand accounts, especially when they talked frankly about the mistakes they had made and the things they would have done differently.

Now to the lessons themselves.

Lesson 1: Leaders Should Be Led by the Group's Needs

On the first day of our journey, we departed from Lukla by midmorning, wending our way along village homes, terraced fields, and valley walls. The trail, which was the sole path to Mount Everest from our direction, was so steep and narrow along its many miles that hikers, porters, and yaks had to carry all gear and provisions required for the journey. By late afternoon, we arrived at our campsite, nestled in a deep valley with a roaring stream nearby and icy peaks above.

That evening, we presented shirts emblazoned with a trek logo to each of the 25 Sherpas who would be our trail guides and yak herders in the days ahead. The act was more than just a token gesture. Each of us was now part of a team, and the success of our expedition would depend greatly on how well we worked with one another. Often, that would mean subjugating one's own needs to those of the group, and we discussed how it was especially important that leaders not let their own interests cloud their judgment when making decisions that would ultimately affect everyone.

Several days later, this principle was brought home to me in a very personal way. An American whom we had met on the trail walked into our campsite at dusk. We had pitched our tents far above the timberline at 14,150 feet, the highest campsite of the trip. Our unexpected visitor reported that her brother was showing the classic symptoms of altitude sickness: nausea, dizziness, and an uncertain gait. If untreated, we knew it could become fatal, but the only sure treatment was to walk him down to a far lower altitude. That would have been harrowing, however, since night was falling and the descent with the stricken hiker would take hours.

Fortunately, our physician for the trek, a graduate of our executive MBA program who specialized in emergency medicine, had packed a full load of medicine. She advised treating the suffering trekker and placing him on an hourly watch to ensure that his symptoms did not worsen during the night. She anticipated that with the early light of dawn, he would be able to walk himself safely down to a lower altitude.

The unexpected encounter raised several conflicting concerns. First, the brother and sister were the children of one of my colleagues at Wharton. Because of that connection, I felt compelled to walk down with the ailing trekker that night to be absolutely sure that his condition didn't deteriorate. But second, I was also responsible for the well-being of my own group, and I knew I had to keep that responsibility uppermost in mind. And third, I was myself exhausted by the day's doings, and the last thing I was fit for at that moment was a long nighttime descent. After weighing these competing considerations, I made up my mind to follow our physician's advice, but if the hiker's health declined during the night, I would make the difficult descent with him.

Fortunately, our doctor had it right: The young man weathered the night, and the next morning he was able to walk himself down to a safer altitude. Several days later, we found him fully recovered in the thicker air of the region's main trading village at 11,300 feet. The incident strengthened my own resolve to keep personal interests from taking precedence over what was best for all.

This concept was reinforced each day of the journey. As our trekkers took turns being leaders for the day, they gained a deeper appreciation of how difficult it can be to put the needs of the group first. Like everyone else, the leaders for the day arrived late in the afternoon at our camp, dog-tired, famished, and sometimes chilled. Their primary responsibility, however, was to ensure that everybody arrived safely, and they had to tend to the immediate needs of others before addressing their own. Placing team needs ahead of one's own can be an abstract concept, but it is put to a primal test when a person is hungry, tired, and cranky. Being the last to eat and the last to sleep helped drive this lesson home. Each of us had to rise to the occasion no matter how miserable we might have felt.

When leaders truly serve and subordinate their private welfare to that of all others, their authority often becomes unquestionable.

In business, executives and managers are frequently tempted to put their own careers first. They may let their egos cloud their thinking or find convenient ways to rationalize decisions that are based purely on their own interests. They may also lose sight of the needs of their teams, bending over backwards to please their bosses or single-mindedly focusing on shareholder demands. Ultimately, though, much of the strength of an organization depends on leaders who are concerned with doing what is best for their followers.

Days later, that lesson was driven home in an unexpected way when we reached a monastery that is home to the spiritual leader for the region's largely Buddhist population. By arrangement, we were able to receive a private audience with the high monk, the reincarnate lama. With the aid of interpreters, we engaged in a freewheeling discussion of Buddhist concepts of leadership. The high monk left us with two indelible affirmations. First, leadership is built by serving. Second, when leaders truly serve and subordinate their private welfare to that of all others, their authority often becomes unquestionable.

Lesson 2: Inaction Can Sometimes Be the Most Difficult—But Wisest—Action

As darkness descended on our high campsite at 14,150 feet—higher than the summit of Colorado's Pikes Peak—our discussion focused on the next day's big event. We were to rise at 2 AM to depart for a long hike to the highest point of our trek, a rocky crag called Chukhung Ri some three and a half miles above sea level. The climb required no ropes, but we knew it would demand strength of will: The distance would be daunting and the air thin. Each of us was privately wondering if we had what it would take—not only to reach the summit but, more important, to back away if the circumstances dictated.

Pondering that issue, we turned our discussion to Arlene Blum, who led an all-women's expedition to climb Annapurna, considered one of the most dangerous peaks in the Himalayas. In the mid-1970s, Blum had tried to join other expeditions but was denied membership because her presence would allegedly undercut the male camaraderie deemed so important for success. So she decided to organize her own team of ten women to reach the summit of the 26,545-foot mountain, the world's tenth highest.

Blum recruited well: Each of her climbers was a world-class mountaineer with a fierce determination to reach the summit. But even if everything went well, not all of them would make it to the top. Expedition mountaineering requires a massive team effort to establish a route and move supplies up the mountain so that on the final day a small group can make the ultimate push to the top. If just one person reaches the summit, all members bask in the glory of that success. This stands in sharp contrast to the recent advent of commercial mountaineering, whose goal is to place all the paying clients on the summit, with success credited only to those who actually stand on top.

On October 15, 1978, after an arduous push from a high camp, two of Blum's team made it to the summit. It was a crowning moment for the group, for women, and for mountaineering: The whole world had been waiting to see if Blum's expedition could equal the accomplishment of the all-men's French team that had been the first to ascend Annapurna in 1950.

A day later, however, two other members of Blum's expedition wanted to reach the summit themselves. At first Blum resisted because her team had already achieved its objective of placing at least one member on top, and the expedition would gain little if others repeated that feat. But the two climbers insisted they be given a chance. Finally, Blum relented. Two days later, the bodies of the two mountaineers were found below the summit, evidence pointing to a fatal fall.

Without a driving urge to succeed, Blum's team would not have been able to move the supplies up the mountain, and the first two climbers would likely have had to stop short of their goal. But the team also needed an equally keen awareness of risk among all of its members.

The second two climbers pushed that envelope too far, forever marring what would otherwise have been a brilliant accomplishment.

As we turned to our own challenge for the next day, our discussion revolved around the same two polar concerns. Many of us were eager to climb to the highest possible point, and we knew that would require all the mental and physical reserves we could summon. At the same time, we told ourselves that without an objective appraisal of our own limitations and of the potential perils of the hike, we ran the risk of allowing our desire to reach that goal to recklessly overwhelm our good judgment, possibly endangering ourselves and others.

Tempering the desire for action in business is likewise difficult. Many executives have been promoted precisely because of their instinct for decisive action. They have been rewarded for being able to pull the trigger when others can't, to fund a risky but potentially lucrative project, or to fire an underperforming manager. Often, though, doing nothing is the wisest course if the alternative is to act precipitously. And not only must leaders keep an eye on themselves, they must also dissuade others from rash decisions.

The next day's hike promised a once-in-a-lifetime opportunity to view the Himalayas from a spectacular vantage point. But the risks were significant: a long, rocky, steep trail with several particularly demanding stretches. With that information in hand, several in our party wisely decided that they would not attempt to reach the high point. Instead, they would accompany us for only part of the hike, stopping on a ridge at 17,000 feet.

At 3:00 the next morning, we started off across the dark terrain, our headlamps bobbing along the trail, giving the appearance of a pearl necklace snaking its way up

the mountainside. Those who had decided against trying
to reach the high point arrived at the 17,000-foot
turnaround location by midmorning and returned safely
back to camp by midafternoon.

The rest of us pushed farther up to the high point of
18,238 feet on Chukhung Ri, arriving by noon at one of
the most stunning vistas in the world. Gigantic glaciers
flowed below on both sides, huge peaks soared in front,
and a mammoth ice wall of the world's third highest
mountain rose just behind. As we emerged from the total
concentration of climbing to finally look around, we
marveled in silence at the majestic view.

Later, a few people who had initially underestimated
their abilities to reach that summit but were encouraged
by their teammates to try for it remarked on how grate-
ful they were to have been pushed beyond what they
thought they were capable of. They had gained a firsthand appreciation for the role that others can play in
helping people overcome their personal doubts and fears
to fulfill their potential.

But for those who are instinctive risk takers, as most
leaders are, tempering that inclination can be extremely
difficult. A few days earlier, as we were heading for our
high camp, one person in the group became dizzy and
disoriented. Even so, he insisted that he was fine, and
others encouraged him to go on. Later, his altitude sickness worsened. Still, he continued to believe that he
could make it. The chief executive of a small industrial
company, he was not used to sitting on the sidelines. But
others on the team had become worried about his safety.
Finally, after a long discussion with a group of us, he
agreed that he should turn back with one of the guides
and rejoin us when we returned to a lower elevation. The

conversation leading up to that decision was difficult and time consuming, but I believe that everyone involved learned from it. For me, it reinforced the idea that although leaders need to help people go for the highest achievement of which they are capable, they must also be keenly aware of the hazards ahead and take the necessary—and sometimes unappealing—steps to avert too grave a risk.

Lesson 3: If Your Words Don't Stick, You Haven't Spoken

Upon our return from Chukhung Ri to the high camp, we were elated by our sense of victory, if utterly spent by the price of achieving it. Many knew that the 18,238 foot summit would most likely be the highest point on which they would ever stand.

The next day had been set aside to give people time to recover. Some worked on their diaries; others opted to do nothing. But several in the group hiked to nearby vistas, such as a lake on the slopes of Ama Dablam, a Matterhorn-like spire jutting above us. I, along with four hikers and two guides, decided to walk toward the base camp of Mount Everest.

By early afternoon, we reached a tiny settlement called Lobuche, perched alongside the enormous Khumbu glacier upon which the camp is located. After a brief rest, we decided to return to our own camp by crossing the glacier, a mile-wide jumble of loose rock and precipitous slopes. The hike across proved very tedious, and we were still on the trail when everyone else was back at camp at 6 PM, the scheduled time for dinner. Alarmed by the possibility of an injury or worse, the day leaders at our camp dispatched a group of Sherpas with hot tea to find us before dark. We met them just 30 minutes from camp and were back before dinner was over.

At first, people were greatly relieved that we had returned safely, but after confirming that we were all fine, their mood changed to anger. Several criticized me for not communicating my plans better. "We didn't know where you were," one said. "We needed more information about what might have been causing your delay. Without that, it was difficult to decide whether to send a rescue party or to wait."

Initially, I was defensive. When I had left that morning, I had firm plans in mind, and I thought I had communicated them to several others over breakfast. But now I realized that I must have just casually mentioned the possibility of crossing the Khumbu glacier because nobody could recall my mention of it by the time they realized we were missing. And, more important, I had not

When leaders make their strategic intent abundantly clear, others know what to do without requiring myriad further instructions.

stated clearly that they shouldn't worry if we weren't back by 6 PM, since crossing the glacier might make us late for dinner. Unwittingly, I had become a textbook example of how *not* to communicate.

In trying to rectify the situation, the worst thing I could have done would have been to downplay my errors, which would have sent the wrong message about how we all needed to communicate. To make sure I didn't do that, I explicitly reviewed what I should have done, and I apologized to everyone for the mistakes I had made. Regardless of what had been said during breakfast, I was ultimately responsible for making sure that the day leaders knew about my plans. My failure to do so not only caused our team to become unnecessarily alarmed, it also resulted in unnecessary work for our Sherpa guides.

Business managers often make the same mistake, failing to grasp the crucial distinction between telling people something and delivering that information so that it really sticks. Indeed, poor communication is one reason why many companies that have devised brilliant strategies fail miserably in executing them. When leaders make their strategic intent abundantly clear—as Wal-Mart's management has in proclaiming its strategy of "low prices, every day"—employees know what to do without requiring myriad further instructions. Achieving that clarity, however, is often far more difficult than managers appreciate.

Although my missteps did not have dire consequences for our group, poor communication did lead to disastrous events on Mount Everest on May 10, 1996. On that ill-fated day, described in the best-seller *Into Thin Air,* a freak blizzard caught dozens of hikers near the summit, killing eight.

During the weeks of preparation for their trek, commercial team leaders Rob Hall and Scott Fischer repeatedly told their clients about the "two o'clock rule." On the day they would attempt to reach the summit, they would have to do so by 2 PM; otherwise they'd have to turn around even if they were within sight of the top. The rationale was clear: Climbers needed time to descend and reach the high camp before nightfall, where the relative security of their tents, sleeping bags, and oxygen could protect them. If they failed to reach camp by dark, they could die on the exposed ridge where windchills can plunge to 100 degrees below zero.

Although Hall and Fischer repeatedly emphasized the two o'clock rule, they evidently failed to do so persuasively. Many of the 33 climbers who had left the high camp just after midnight on May 10 were still pressing for the summit after 2 PM, and Hall and Fischer themselves did not reach the top until well after that time. The consequences were tragic. After 5 PM, when all the climbers should have been crawling into their life-protecting tents back at the high camp, a violent storm hit the mountain and killed five climbers in the party (and three others on the Tibetan side of Mount Everest) caught in the open, including both Hall and Fischer.

Lesson 4: Leading Upwards Can Feel Wrong When It's Right

One of the most magnificent settings of our trek was Tengboche, a ridge at 12,670 feet that is the home of the region's best-known monastery. With a commanding view of Mount Everest, Tengboche has long been a stopping point for virtually everyone on their way to Everest.

It was at this location that the final, equally powerful lesson was driven home. We had been debating the events of *Into Thin Air,* and among our questions was whether one of the commercial clients, Beck Weathers, might have averted the disaster that nearly resulted in his death. On his way up the summit ridge, Weathers became temporarily blind, and his team leader, Rob Hall, instructed him to stay put until Hall returned from the summit to lead him safely down to the high camp.

But Weathers failed to ask Hall to elaborate on his terse instruction, and as a result Weathers spent the entire day waiting for his leader to return. Caught in the killer storm later that afternoon, Hall never did come down, and Weathers's resulting delay in descending left him badly exposed when the storm hit. After he lost consciousness, others left him for dead. He somehow survived the storm but suffered grievous frostbite on his hands and face. In retrospect, had Weathers pressed Hall, his superior on the expedition, for more information, they could have developed a contingency plan: If Hall wasn't back by an agreed-upon time, then Weathers should head down with another guide or teammate.

After much discussion about Weathers, our ongoing debate was aided by a serendipitous encounter. Along the Tengboche ridge, we happened to meet another of the principals who had miraculously survived the 1996 disaster, Sandy Hill Pittman. She and Weathers had been among the many clients who had left the high camp at 26,000 feet just past midnight on May 10. Having already debated the events of that fateful day, and with the summit of Mount Everest on our horizon, we asked Pittman if there was anything she would have done differently. Her response was unexpected.

Pittman's guide, Scott Fischer, had moved slowly toward the summit during the early morning hours of May 10. She had recognized that he was off his game, but she said nothing as they headed for the summit. She was too focused on her own ascent and too confident in Fischer to worry about his condition. Later that day, however, as the storm enveloped the mountain, Fischer sat down on the way back and never stood up.

Pittman told us that she wished she had done more to help him. Earlier on their expedition, Fischer had insisted that his clients build teamwork among themselves to ensure that they would assist one another during a crisis, and his demand proved lifesaving for Pittman, who was rescued from the storm by her team members. But she had not done enough for Fischer. His leadership had saved her life, she said, but hers had fallen short in saving his.

Pittman's frank assessment of her actions helped bring home the notion that leadership is not just about mobilizing those below; it's also about marshaling the people above. After all, everyone is fallible, and even the most experienced CEOs and other top executives have blind spots. Our responsibility, then, is to help them avoid the pitfalls that they haven't seen. Of course, leading upwards often feels wrong because of the hierarchical culture prevalent in most companies, and it requires tremendous diplomacy and tact to avoid a political blunder that can derail or end a promising career. At the same time, many great companies have foundered because of faulty decisions made at the top while middle managers sat on their hands. The harrowing experience of Weathers and Pittman—and the difference that upward leadership might have made for them and for Scott Fischer that day—stands as a forceful reminder for keeping this leadership principle in mind. In effect, we all need to be ready to lead even when we are not in charge.

At the end of our journey, we spent our final evening together in Kathmandu, recapping the various things we learned, both from our achievements and from our mistakes. We were tanner and fitter—and noticeably thinner—than we were when we first arrived in Nepal two weeks earlier. We were also more aware that good leadership requires many capabilities and actions, and we had a deeper, fuller appreciation of what it really takes to lead.

During our trek, we had hiked some 40,000 vertical feet, and we had gazed upon four of the world's six highest summits. Humbled by our own experiences and by those of other trekkers in the Himalayas, we realized more than ever that mastering leadership is an ongoing journey. Indeed, as difficult as our hike up the lower slopes of Mount Everest was, the harder work would commence as we applied the principles of good leadership to our management responsibilities in the years ahead.

Originally published in October 2001
Reprint R0109B

Followership

It's Personal, Too

ROBERT GOFFEE AND GARETH JONES

T HE ARTICLES IN THIS SPECIAL ISSUE bear lucid testimony to the fact that leadership has endured as *the* burning issue for all kinds of organizations—and for executives themselves as they grapple to define their personal successes (or lack thereof) in business. But to be adequately understood, leadership must be seen for what it is: part of a duality or a relationship. There can be no leaders without followers.

So let's end this compendium by looking at this incendiary topic through the follower's eyes. We're lucky; the sociological and psychological literature on the follower's experience is rich indeed. It tells us that people seek, admire, and respect—that is, they follow—leaders who produce within them three emotional responses.

The first is a feeling of significance. Followers will give their hearts and souls to authority figures who say, "You really matter," no matter how small the followers' contributions may be. This dynamic, of course, comes from the human drive to be valued. We yearn to not live and die in vain. When leaders, then, herald the significance of an individual's work, they are rewarded with loyalty, even obedience. They have given meaning to a follower's life, and as a basis for a relationship, that is not just sturdy; it is as solid as cement.

The second emotional response followers want from their leaders is a feeling of community. Now there's a messy concept—community. The library is filled with books trying to define it. But for our purposes, let's say community occurs when people feel a unity of purpose around work and, simultaneously, a willingness to relate to one another as human beings. It is the rare business executive who can create such an environment. But you can be sure that when a feeling of community is successfully engineered, it is so deeply gratifying that followers will call the person who created it their leader.

Finally, followers will tell you that a leader is nearby when they get a buzzing feeling. People want excitement, challenge, and edge in their lives. It makes them feel engaged in the world. And so, despite all the literature that tells you a leader needn't be charismatic, followers will sooner feel leadership from someone who is extroverted and energetic than from someone who isn't. Right or wrong, that's how followers feel. Some traditional theories of leadership portray the follower as an empty vessel waiting to be led, or even transformed, by the leader. Other theories suggest that followers require nurturing and need to be persuaded to give of themselves. But these theories would have us believe that followers are passive. Yes, followership implies commitment, but never without conditions. The follower wants the leader to create feelings of significance, community, and excitement—or the deal is off.

After all, to the follower, as much as it is to the person who stands above him in the organizational hierarchy, leadership is entirely personal.

Originally Published in December 2001
Reprint R0111L

About the Contributors

RICHARD BOYATZIS is professor of organizational behavior and chair of the department of organizational behavior at the Weatherhead School of Management at Case Western Reserve University. Prior to joining the faculty at CWRU, he was president and CEO of McBer & Co., Chief Operating Officer of Yankelovich, Skelly & White, and a board member of the Hay Group. Boyatzis is the author of numerous articles on human motivation, self-directed behavior change, leadership, managerial competencies, and a research book entitled *The Competent Manager*. He is also the author of *Transforming Qualitative Information*, and coauthor of *Innovations in Professional Education* with S.S. Cowen and D.A. Kolb. His most recent book, *Primal Leadership*, was coauthored with Daniel Goleman and Annie McKee.

HARRIS COLLINGWOOD is a senior editor at the *Harvard Business Review*.

ROBERT GOFFEE is professor of organizational behavior at London Business School. He also serves as deputy dean for executive education, director of the Innovation Exchange, and a member of the Governing Body. Previously, he was director of the Accelerated Development Programme and chair of the Organisational Behaviour Group. Professor Goffee has led significant executive development initiatives in Europe, North America, and Asia. His work has covered a range of industries

with a focus on leadership, change, and corporate performance. His clients have included Heineken, Roche, Sonae,
KPMG, Unilever, and MLIM. He has published nine books and
over fifty articles in the areas of entrepreneurship, managerial
careers, organization design, and corporate culture. These
include *Entrepreneurship in Europe, Reluctant Managers, Corporate Realities,* and *The Character of a Corporation,* coauthored with Gareth Jones. His recent article in *Harvard
Business Review,* coauthored with Gareth Jones, "Why Should
Anyone Be Led By You?" won the McKinsey Award for best
article published in 2000. He is a founding partner of Creative
Management Associates, which consults to major international companies around the world in the areas of change
management, top teams, and organizational development.

DANIEL GOLEMAN is author of the best-selling books *Emotional Intelligence* and *Working with Emotional Intelligence*
and coauthor of the forthcoming *Primal Leadership.* A trained
psychologist, he worked for many years for the *New York
Times,* covering the brain and behavioral sciences. He has also
been a visiting faculty member at Harvard University. Dr.
Goleman is co-chair of the Consortium for Research on Emotional Intelligence in Organizations at Rutgers University and
a founder of the Collaborative for Social and Emotional
Learning at the University of Illinois at Chicago. He consults
on leadership and organizational development worldwide.

GARETH JONES began his career as an academic in economic and social studies at the University of East Anglia
before moving to the London Business School, where he
joined the Organisational Behaviour Group. During this
period he directed the School's Accelerated Development
Programme. However, the attractions of a "real" job in business proved too great, and he joined Polygram, then the
world's largest recorded music company. Appointed to senior
vice president for Polygram's global human resources, his

responsibilities covered more than thirty countries. In 1996 he returned to academia when he became the B.T. Professor of Organisational Development at Henley and served on the Board of Governors. His most recent job was as director of human resources and internal communications at the BBC, and he is currently a visiting professor at INSEAD and a founding partner of Creative Management Associates (CMA), a consultancy focused on organizations where creativity is a source of competitive strength. Mr. Jones' research interests include organizational design, culture, leadership, and change. He is author of several books, including *The Character of a Corporation* with Robert Goffee. His articles have appeared in journals such as the *European Management Journal, Human Relations,* and *Harvard Business Review,* and his recent *Harvard Business Review* article, "Why Should Anyone Be Led by You?", coauthored with Robert Goffee, won the McKinsey Award for best article published in 2000.

JULIA KIRBY is a senior editor at *Harvard Business Review* and has developed articles on a wide range of topics, from managing creativity to spotting creative accounting. She also oversees the magazine's Case Study department. Prior to joining *HBR,* she worked in the management consulting industry for fifteen years as a researcher, writer, and editor.

DR. ANNIE MCKEE serves on the faculty of the University of Pennsylvania, teaches at the Wharton School's Aresty Institute of Executive Education, and is a principal in the Teleos Leadership Institute, an international management consulting firm. In these roles, she works around the globe with senior executives as an advisor, focusing on leadership and organizational transformation. Prior to founding the Teleos Institute, Dr. McKee was director of management development of the Hay Group, spent several years as the managing director of the Center for Professional Development at the University of Pennsylvania, and taught in the Wharton School

M.B.A. Program. Her research interests focus on leadership, executive development, and organizational change. She has written and presented numerous articles and speeches on subjects including emotional intelligence, organizational change, the development of leadership capabilities, management education, managing an increasingly complex workforce, and action research methodologies. She has also recently completed a book entitled *Primal Leadership* with Daniel Goleman and Richard Boyatzis. She contributes to her field through research, reviewing and editing professional journals, and by providing pro bono services for international nongovernmental agencies and the Philadelphia community. She can be reached at: anniemckee1@aol.com

LIEUTENANT GENERAL WILLIAM G. PAGONIS is the author (with Jeffrey L. Cruikshank) of *Moving Mountains: Lessons in Leadership and Logistics from the Gulf War.*

WILLIAM H. PEACE is managing director of Spirent Communications SW Ltd. (a subsidiary of Spirent plc), an organization engaged in the design and manufacture of satellite navigation development and test equipment. He also works as an independent consultant to management teams and executives. In the early 1990s he worked for a mid-size business performance improvement consultancy and built his own practice around BPR, team-building, and mentoring. He was president of Carrier Corporation's European air-conditioning business and general manager of Westinghouse Electric's synthetic fuels business. He is a graduate of Yale University and lives in England. His particular business interests are management style and organizational culture.

Fortune calls THOMAS J. PETERS the Ur-guru (guru of gurus) of management and compares him to Ralph Waldo Emerson, Henry David Thoreau, Walt Whitman, and H.L.

Mencken. *The Economist* tags him the Uber-guru. And his unconventional views led *BusinessWeek* to describe him as business' "best friend and worst nightmare." Mr. Peters is the author of several best-selling books, including *In Search of Excellence* with Robert H. Waterman, Jr., named by NPR as one of the "Top Three Business Books of the Century," *A Passion for Excellence* with Nancy Austin, *Thriving on Chaos, Liberation Management, The Circle of Innovation, The Tom Peters Seminar,* and *The Pursuit of WOW!*. Mr. Peters' series of books on reinventing work, *The Brand You50, The Project50,* and *The Professional Service Firm50,* were released in September 1999. Mr. Peters presents about 100 major seminars each year, and has recently spoken in Australia, Malaysia, Germany, Turkey, India, Saudi Arabia, South Africa, Thailand, and Ecuador. He has authored hundreds of articles for various newspapers and popular and academic journals, including *BusinessWeek, The Economist, Financial Times,* the *Wall Street Journal,* the *New York Times, Inc., Fast Company,* the *Washington Monthly, California Management Review,* the *Academy of Management Review, ForbesASAP,* and *Harvard Business Review.* Mr. Peters served on active duty in the U.S. Navy in Vietnam and Washington from 1966 to 1970, was a Senior White House Drug Abuse Advisor, and worked at McKinsey & Company, becoming a partner in 1977. He is a fellow of the International Academy of Management, the World Productivity Association, the International Customer Service Association, and the Society for Quality and Participation. He is also the chairman and founder of a global training and consulting company, Tom Peters Company (tompeterscompany!).

RICHARD S. TEDLOW is the Class of 1949 Professor of Business Administration at the Harvard Business School, where he is a specialist in the history of business. Professor Tedlow joined the Harvard Business School faculty in 1979 and from 1979 through 1982 taught first-year marketing. His involvement in marketing has continued, and he has been a member of the faculty of the "Strategic Retail Management Seminar," "Top Management Seminar for Retailers and Suppliers," "Managing Brand Meaning," and "Strategic Marketing Management" executive education programs. From 1978 to the present, he has been involved in the School's business history program. He has also taught in numerous executive programs at the School as well as at corporations, including programs in marketing strategy and general management. His most recent book, *Giants of Enterprise: Seven Business Innovators and the Empires They Built*, was selected by *BusinessWeek* as one of the top ten business books of 2001.

MICHAEL USEEM is William and Jacalyn Egan Professor of Management and director of the Center for Leadership and Change Management at the Wharton School, University of Pennsylvania. He is the author of *Leading Up: How to Lead Your Boss So You Both Win, The Leadership Moment: Nine True Stories of Triumph and Disaster and Their Lessons for Us All, Investor Capitalism: How Money Managers Are Changing the Face of Corporate America, Executive Defense: Shareholder Power and Corporate Reorganization*, and *The Inner Circle: Large Corporations and the Rise of Business Political Activity in the U.S. and U.K.* He also directs the Wharton Leadership Ventures (http://leadership.wharton.upenn.edu/l_change/trips/index.shtml), which includes the annual leadership trek to Mt. Everest.

Index